How To Turbo Charge Your Life
with

Personal Developments
and Smart Investments

Cindy L. Lam

Disclaimer:

This book is for informational purposes only and is not intended to provide legal financial or investment advice. Please seek or consult with professional advisors for any financial or investment decisions.

Library of Congress Control Number: 2025900255

ISBN: 9781966805014 (Paperback)
ISBN: 9781966805021 (Hardcover)
ISBN: 9781966805007 (eBook)

Published by: Royal Empress Empire, LLC

DEDICATION

I dedicate this book to my family for their love and support.

Table of Contents

PART ONE

PERSONAL DEVELOPMENTS

Chapter 1

Your Health is Your Wealth

Health is the #1 most important thing in your life. It is your most valuable asset and resource. Without good health, you can't take care of loved ones, offer help to others, or enjoy a pleasurable life, and you might not have the ability to accomplish all the things you want. There's a Chinese saying, "If you don't have good health, you won't be able to go and pick up even when there's gold just lying on the ground." or something to that effect.

Many times, we take health for granted, especially when we are young. When we are young, we think we are invisible, untouchable or even the thought of taking care of our health as a priority rarely crosses our minds.

However, our health is a result of the cumulative effect. What we do and eat has a significant effect on our body. Are you doing all you can to help you live your best and healthy life?

Let's look at some ways and things we can do to help us live a healthier, stronger, and longer life.

Nutrition and Diet

The types of food you put into your body have a significant effect on the quality of your health. I believe we all know that to some extent. Yet, we have a hard time watching what we eat due to various reasons such as most of the unhealthy foods just taste good, they are easily available or cost less than healthier food.

We have a hard time controlling our cravings. It takes willpower and additional cost to eat healthy food. Take note of what you currently eat daily now. Are you eating enough fruits and vegetables? How about whole grains, nuts, low fat dairy, and protein foods?

It's important that you eat a recommended daily serving in each of these categories. I am not a nutrition expert, so I encourage you to look into the daily intake requirements of these food groups from a reliable source.

Exercise

I am sure you already know that exercise is good for our body and mind. So why don't we do it more often? It's because it requires time, commitment, and willpower to do them.

We always tend to have excuses not to do it such as we are too busy, don't have time for it or will do it tomorrow, etc. I understand that not many people wanted to sign up for a gym membership or buy some expensive equipment.

However, you can get some exercise in many ways. I find exercising at home is the easiest way to get some exercise into your daily schedule. Set aside 15 minutes or 30 minutes in the morning. Do some stretching, low impact aerobics, yoga movements etc.

How about going for a walk in a park? If you enjoy outdoor activities, go for a bike ride, play some tennis, go for a hike. Daily exercise helps improve our moods, blood circulation and just overall well-being.

Be Your Own Advocate for Your Health

No one knows your body better than you, not even your doctors. So many times, we view doctors as someone who has higher power and forget that they are human just like us but with more knowledge regarding how our body works due to their medical studies. We forget that doctors are humans too and have flaws just like us. They can make mistakes such as misdiagnosing an illness, have misjudgments, or bad behaviors, etc.

I would say most doctors in general are good doctors and are genuine in wanting to help their patients. However, I have encountered a great deal of bad doctors as well, and so do many others who have similar experiences.

You can tell some doctors are in this profession simply for the money and don't give a damn about their patients. I can't believe how bad some of the doctors are. I have immigrant parents who don't speak much English, so I am the one who usually takes them to doctor appointments and be their translator.

One time, we went to see this doctor because my mom complains of having pain in the back or other areas. Without doing any examination or asking questions. What the doctor said shocked me, he said **"You are fine, that's how it is when you are old, that's normal to have pain."** I was like what??? And he just kept saying you're fine and dismissed us and that's the end of the office visit. No examination or asking questions like how long the pain lasts, when it starts, are there any other symptoms, etc. NOTHING. I CAN'T BELIEVE IT; it was a complete waste of our time and money. This is a perfect example of how bad some doctors are out there.

I have personally dealt with a fair share of bad doctors too. For example, I changed insurance and signed up with a doctor close to home as my primary doctor.

So, I started going to this new doctor for my health needs. During the office visit, they put you in one of those individual patient rooms where you would be waiting for the doctor to come in to see you.

This doctor of mine, the first thing he did when he opened the door was, he said **"Do we need any blood work today?"** In my mind, I was like what?? How should I know? You have not even taken a look at me yet or asked me what's the reason I am here or examine me and the first thing you ask is, **do we need blood work?** Am I the doctor or are you the doctor? **Unbelievable!**

I don't want to be rude, so I just said I don't know. You haven't looked at me yet to see if it's needed. And he did the same thing the next few visits. The first thing he asked was, "Do we blood work today?" I just can't believe it. Finally, I decided I have given this doctor too many chances and decided to switch doctor.

We have to take charge of our own health, no one is going to do it for us. Whenever we go to see a doctor, I find that many times we can't remember when or how it started and have a hard time describing our pain or symptoms.

I recommend keeping a health journal and recording your symptoms and anything that's unusual. Keep a log of when a symptom starts, how long it lasts, how would you describe the pain, is there anything that you are doing that brought on or triggered the pain or symptom, etc. Learning how to describe your symptoms and pain is crucial to helping the doctors diagnose your illness more accurately.

For example, is this an acute pain (short-term) or chronic pain (lasts more than six months)? Is this a nociceptive pain meaning relating to nociceptors and electrical signals?

Visceral pain is injuries or damage to your internal organs. Visceral pain is usually described as pressure, aching, squeezing, or cramping. Neuropathic pain is due to damage or dysfunction to your nervous system.

Neuropathic pain can be described as burning, freezing, tingling, numbness, stabbing, shooting, etc. Other words you can use to describe your pain might be sharp, dull, prickly, stinging or intense, etc.

We all agree that there are many good doctors out there doing good work. However, we can't ignore the fact that there are bad ones too. I have encountered a few of those bad doctors over the years.

My most recent doctor is one of the best doctors I have ever encountered, very professional, very knowledgeable and skilled at what he's doing, and has good bedside manners. He restored my faith in how I view some doctors.

When it comes to doctors, be your own advocate. Seek second opinions. Do your own research. What a doctor prescribes might work for someone, but it might not work the same for you. Everyone's body reacts differently, so listen to your own body. Don't be afraid to speak up when something is not right in your gut feelings. Ask yourself if this is necessary. Know your pros and cons. Temporary fix vs long term outcome. Are there any alternatives? Do you feel any improvements with the current treatment plan? Etc.

It's important to be your own advocate. The human body is complex. There are still many unknowns. Even the best doctors won't know everything about the human body. So, listen to your own body and be your own advocate.

Managing Stress Level

Our health is not just our body, we must take care of our minds too. The state of our mind has a direct impact on our health. One of the biggest factors that causes many illnesses is **stress**. When we are stressed, our body releases cortisol and other stress hormones which lead to high blood pressure, heart disease, strokes, etc. It also causes digestive problems, headaches, anxiety and many other issues.

To help us better manage our stress levels, we should incorporate meditation into our daily habits. We live in a hectic world; studies have shown that setting aside some quiet time for daily meditation helps calm our mind, reduce stress, increase focus and improve our overall health.

It also helps us to be more mindful and live in the present. There are many other ways or things we can do to help reduce our stress, such as listening to music or going for a walk. I love listening to my favorite or upbeat dance music, it always improves my mood.

One of our biggest sources of stress contributors is the people around us. They can bring their negativity or drama into your life which causes you stress. Learn to surround yourself with uplifting and positive people, limit your exposure to the negative ones.

In today's world, there is a lot of chaos and negative things going on such as geopolitical tensions and social problems. Even though we would like to keep up with what's going on in the world, we should limit our time watching or listening to news.

Most of the time, the news is negative in nature and could have a negative impact on your mood, such as feeling sad or bad for what happened. We can't really do anything or help the situation because it has already happened, knowing about it only impacts our well-being. So, limit your time spent on social media or news outlets.

Are you doing all you can now to prevent or limit future illnesses? Prevention is the key to living a long and enjoyable life. Do your daily habits include exercise, reducing stress and eating a healthy diet?

Remember prevention is better than fixing problems later. Would you rather pay a little extra to eat better and healthier food now or the cost of medical bills later?

Our health is our most precious resource. It should be the number one priority for all of us. It is the most important thing as human beings. Money can improve it but can't buy it. If you ask many millionaires who have passed away to trade all their money for another 5 or 10 years. They would gladly trade their money to live for a few more years but they can't. So, take good care of your health. Your health is your wealth. Prevention is the key. No one can do it for you. It's up to you.

Chapter 2

Master Your Mind

Why do some millionaires feel unhappy about their life despite having everything while someone who doesn't have much is very happy with their life? It is because our mind determines our state of being. What we feel and think is all in our mind. Learning how to master your mind is the key to a happier and fulfilling life by harnessing the power of your thoughts.

Our mind lies within our brains, which is our central command. It dictates how we feel and think. Mastering your mind is like taking control of a spaceship, you guide it where you want to go and how to get there (Sabater, 2023).

It is a powerful tool, and it has capabilities that no other species possess except for us humans. Inside our brain, there are vast pathways and networks like superhighways.

The brain has the capacity to rewire itself and find new pathways called Neuroplasticity. Scientists have yet to understand and uncover all its secrets (Sabater, 2023).

The brain is made up of billions of cells called neurons. These neurons constantly send electrical and chemical signals, these activities are called neurotransmitters which pass our thoughts, memories, and emotions (Cherry, 2023).

The brain and mind are connected as one working unit. Yet, there's a distinction between the two. The brain is a physical matter, where you can see and touch (like in a lab environment).

The brain regulates your movements, heart beats, breathing, etc. The mind on the other hand is mental, you can't touch or see it. The mind is your thoughts, your emotions, your dreams, your consciousness, your memories.

The mind deals with things like reasoning, logic, creativity, self-awareness, and solving complex problems, etc. The brain can deteriorate over time due to cells weakening or dying off. The mind however can continue to grow and develop and learn new skills and gain wisdoms way into your old age.

Our mind is constantly bombarded with all sorts of thoughts. It could be filled with positive or negative thoughts throughout the day. The mind has a mind of its own, it auto fills anything that comes to mind. Whatever is on your mind affects your mood and how you feel.

When you put emphasis on a particular thought, it magnifies. That's why it's important to fill your mind with positive and constructive thoughts.

So how do you control your thoughts? The key is to be MINDFUL of your thoughts. Whenever a negative thought pops up, ask yourself why does this thought come up, does it have any merit? Then replace it with something positive.

For example, you have a presentation tomorrow and a thought of you messing up comes up. You ask yourself, am I over worrying? You are well prepared and know your materials and have done a lot of practice. You feel confident that you will do well, so this thought has no merits. Replace it with you are going to do great because you are well prepared.

Our minds are powerful. It can be filled with sunshine and happiness or doom and gloom. Change the way you think, and your world changes with it. You can be in a prison and still find joy and meaning in life like Viktor Frankl, who is the author of the bestselling book, "Man's Search for Meaning". Whereas someone who lives in a mansion can still feel depressed.

Our dreams and goals begin with a thought or an idea. It's from that initial thought or idea along with a written plan containing steps and taking consistent actions that bring our dreams and goals into reality in the real world.

The mind has two levels, awareness level and subconscious level. When we are aware of our thoughts and emotions, that's the first level. The second level is our subconscious mind.

The subconscious mind is where we store all our long-term memories, habits, strong emotions, etc. It acts like a memory bank. It stores strong emotions, childhood memories or traumas, something that is repeated often such as a habit. It stores memories and experiences long after the conscious mind has forgotten about them (Sabater, 2023).

The subconscious mind operates in an autopilot mode. Your gut feeling comes from your subconscious mind because it processes information based on your experiences throughout life and provides you with intuitive insights and guides you with decision-making processes.

When you do something without thinking or act in autopilot mode, such as brushing your teeth every morning. That action is ingrained in your subconscious. Repeated actions are wired into your subconscious.

Many people try to hack the subconscious to help achieve their dreams and goals through methods such as daily meditation and repeating daily positive affirmations. By repeating these positive affirmations, it will be ingrained into our subconscious which in turn guide your actions and attract positive energy and circumstance that align with your dreams and goals.

Rather we are aware of it or not, we emit certain energy or vibrations out to the world and on a subconscious level. The more positive our vibrations are, the better things and opportunities we will attract. In turn, they will affect our mood, our actions and our lives.

Our mind is subjective and based on personal experiences. How we feel and think is personal to each of us. You can have two people watching the same movie but have two different reactions and experiences. Our mind and perceptions are shaped by our own experiences and the environments we are in.

The bottom line is your mind is powerful. What you think about matters a lot. The quality of your thoughts determines the quality of your life. That's why it's important to be mindful of your thoughts. Practice mindfulness daily.

Be aware of your negative thoughts. Most of our negative thoughts stem from over-thinking, fear of something or fear of the unknown, worries, stress from work, finances or relationships, etc.

Learn to reframe these thoughts, if something we have no control over it, let them go. 99% of the time our fears and worries have no merits or any chance of happening. The more we learn to replace our negative thoughts with positive and uplifting thoughts; the less space your mind has for the negative ones.

Your thoughts have the ability to shape your life. If you want to live a more positive life, your thoughts have to be matched up. So today, make up your mind to be happy and think positive thoughts and be mindful of what goes into your mind.

Chapter 3

Go After Your Dreams and Goals

Have you ever dreamt of traveling around the world or starting your own business? These are just two examples of dreams and goals some people might have. What are some of your dreams and goals? What are you going to do about them? Are you currently working on them, making plans, or taking steps to achieve them? What are some hurdles or difficulties that prevent you from making them a reality? Is it time or money or both?

Goal setting is an important part of life if you want to make the most of it. Otherwise, you are just drifting in life and not achieving anything meaningful to you. Write down all the goals you wanted to achieve, then set a timeline of when you wanted to achieve them, they need to be specific, measurable, and achievable.

Ask yourself what personal goals you want to achieve. You can list your personal goals such as eating healthier, losing weight, or learning some new skills, etc.

How about your financial goals? Do you want to be able to retire early or have financial freedom or own your own home?

Work on the goals that have the greatest impact on your life first. The 80 /20 rule, also known as the Pareto Principle. It means prioritizing the 20% factors that will generate the best results or 80% outcomes.

To make any dreams and goals a reality, a solid plan is needed. Goal setting plans need to have actionable steps, have a timeline, and are achievable.

For example, say you wanted to open a new restaurant. Do you know how much it will cost? Are you going to finance it, or do you have enough savings to do so? Have you considered the cost associated with it, such as rent, labor cost, utilities, insurance, etc.?

Do you have a location in mind where you wanted to open up at? How soon do you want to open it? In six months or a year? Are you going to lease or buy an existing restaurant? What type of food do you want to serve?

Have you done any research to see what competitions you have around the location you're planning to open in? Is your type of food popular with the customers in the area? You got to know your customer base and do a cost analysis in order to be successful.

Do you have a marketing plan to attract customers to your restaurant? These are the types of things that you need to think about and plan out and to take the necessary steps to achieve them. If you don't have a solid plan, it will be just a wish on your list.

Roadblocks of Goal Setting

Now let's look at some of the hurdles that prevent many people from achieving their goals. What I find the biggest hurdles are lack of self-discipline, the tendency to procrastinate, or lack of motivation. Also, other factors such as our self-limiting beliefs and the fear of failure, etc. I, myself, am guilty of the things mentioned above too sometimes.

As humans, we tend to avoid doing hard tasks whenever possible. Achieving goals or doing hard tasks requires self-discipline, commitment of time and resources.

Say you wanted to lose 25 lbs. Then you must set time aside to do exercise and eat a healthy diet. In the beginning, you might commit to doing 30 minutes of exercise each morning. After a week or two into it, you find yourself struggling to keep that commitment. By the third week, you already lose motivation to do it.

To achieve your goals, you will need to work at them consistently every day and motivate yourself to work at them and to remind yourself why this goal is important and how it will improve your life. When faced with a hard task, we tend to put them off or procrastinate, it's just easier to do. We always have some excuses; I will just do them tomorrow. Then tomorrow comes and you have another excuse. Pretty soon, a month has passed by, and you are nowhere near your goals.

Achieving goals requires an upfront price of sacrificing time and resources, which many people are not willing to pay to get the reward. Many people want many things, but they don't want to put in the hard work or commitment and expect to have things handed to them. It just doesn't work that way. You might get lucky and get the things you wanted without hard work.

For example, you always wanted to own a dream car, such as a nice red Ferrari sports car, which costs a lot of money. Say you have rich parents, and they decided to gift you with your dream car for your birthday. Sure, it's nice to get it as a gift, but had you bought the car with your own money from the money you earned from working or investing. I assure you that you will feel a sense of achievement and feel proud to own that car and take better care of it.

Another hurdle preventing people from achieving their goals is fear of failure. We all have the nagging thought, what if it doesn't work out. What if I fail and disappoint my family. View failures as a steppingstone to your goals. You will gain and learn valuable knowledge and skills in the process.

You learn what works and what doesn't and do better next time. There's a famous quote by Thomas Edison, the famous inventor, that goes like this "I have not failed. I've found 10,000 ways that won't work". Another one is "Many of life's failures are people who did not realize how close they were to success when they gave up". So don't give up, learn from them. Overcome your fears. Think of the worst-case scenario and the outcome is something you can handle. 99% of the time, the fears in our mind don't materialize. So, take steps to overcome your fears. If you consistently work at it, you will achieve your goals.

Make the decision to achieve your goals today no matter how small or big, start working on them if you haven't already. Create a written plan with steps to take and actions to achieve them. Without a written plan, they are just wishes. Break tasks into smaller steps. Set a deadline, without a timeline, it just doesn't get done. Overcome your procrastination tendencies or excuses.

Make a commitment to work on them every day. If you do these things, you will find yourself closer to your goals each day and before you know it, you have achieved your goals when it seems insurmountable in the beginning.

So, I encourage you to go after your dreams and goals today and live your best life!!

Chapter 4

Time Management

What do Elon Musk, Warren Buffet and you have in common? It is that we are human and have the same 24 hours a day. Just because they're rich, they don't get any more time in a day than you do. They might delegate and get more time to do other things but still have the same 24 hours. We are all given 24 hours a day, rich or poor. It is how you use it that makes a difference.

TIME is one of the most precious and valuable resources we have as human beings, the same as health. Even though we have the same 24 hours, why do some people get so much more done than we do? The key is planning and time management. Without proper planning and managing your time effectively, before you know it, a day, a week, a year has passed without you accomplishing the things that you wanted to get done. And then you wondered, where has time gone?

So, how do you make better use of your time? Let's start by listing the things that you wanted to accomplish such as your short-term and long-term goals. Also think of what you want to get out of life and what's important to you.

Next is to break them down into small actionable tasks and what you need to do to achieve those goals. Give it a specific timeline of when you want them to be accomplished. For example, if you want to lose 25 lbs. in 3 months' time frame. You need to come up with an exercise plan such as exercising 30 minutes each morning around 6:00 am before work and eating a healthy diet, etc.

So, what are some ways to manage your time effectively? For me, I like to list all things that I wanted to accomplish. It doesn't matter if it's short-term or long-term, just list them all and add any new ones. Then I would put them into different categories. Urgent but low priorities. High priorities but not urgent, meaning it doesn't have to be done right away but they are important to get done. High priorities are things or actions that have positive effects or improve your life. Then I have another category for Other/Misc or social activities.

To better organize tasks or things that need to get done, I would create a to-do list for the week and for the day. We all live a busy life and can't always remember all the things that we have to do or need to get done. Each week, I plan and list what I must do and what I want to get done. Then, I would create a daily to-do list for a particular day. It's important to create the to-do list the day before so you have an idea of what's coming up and if any extra preparation is needed.

The actions or tasks listed are not set in stone and can be adjusted as needed on the day. What doesn't get done will carry over to the next day. For example, on your Mondays to do list, you wanted to go pick up your dry-cleaning clothes but got sidetracked, but you have time on Tuesday, so you put that on Tuesday's list.

To me, having a to-do list helps tremendously to get things done. As you all know, most people are very busy and forgetful. List them out helps free up your mind.

Also, for things like doctor appointments and events coming up that you know the date. Put them in your calendar. Most phones have a calendar, put the detail and time in them so the phone will send you a reminder.

Today, we live in a fast-paced world with lots of distractions and demands that chip away our time. Now, let's look at some ways to manage your time more effectively.

Manage Your Distractions

Today, we are living in a world full of distractions and things that chip away your time and concentration. We spend hours and hours scrolling mindlessly on social media such as Facebook, Tik Tok, Instagram etc.

These social media platforms are designed to keep you addicted and hooked without you realizing the amount of time you are spending on them and before you know it, an hour or two has gone by. Whereas you could have used that time to do something that's productive to your life. We are all guilty of that, including myself, because they can be addictive and entertaining. The key is to be aware of it and limit your time spent on these platforms.

Another area where your time is demanded is the people around you, rather it is your family, your co-workers/boss, or your friends, or heck even your neighbors sometimes. I won't necessarily categorize all of them as distractions but rather as time that is required from you. They all wanted a piece of you, especially if you have something or skill that will help them.

Of course, your family should be your highest priority and taking care of them in all forms is important. Things such as taking kids to soccer games, making sure they are well cared for, and are healthy (doctor appointments), etc. all require your time.

Managing your time with family also requires planning your day. When possible, try delegating tasks or sharing tasks with another family member. Condense trips such as laundry pickup while doing grocery shopping, etc.

If you have a regular job, there goes your 8 hours plus commute time. Nowadays, many people have the option of working from home. So, you might save some commute time. At work, you can face many distractions too, such as when your co-workers decide to stop by, rather it's for a casual chat or work related, it interrupts or distracts you from what you are doing, or your boss decides he/she needs a certain report right now.

To get a better handle of your day at work, prioritize your work, limit your distractions from co-workers, limit your chats to brief moments, or politely let them know you can't chat right now because you have a deadline to meet.

Friends are an important part of life, rather they are close friends or just acquaintances. The quality of the people you surround yourself with has a profound impact on your life. So, choose your friends wisely. So how do friends and acquaintances impact your time? Building a good friendship requires you to spend time with them, to get to know them and perhaps do activities together. To make better use of your time regarding friends, choose quality friends.

Choose friends that are mutually beneficial. Choose people who uplift you instead of people who constantly bring drama into your life. Limit your time with people who drain your energy or people who constantly ask for favors but never offer any in return.

Remember your time is valuable, time is your life, don't give it away freely just because you know them. Whenever someone asks you for a favor. Ask yourself these questions, is this person important to me? Do they truly need help? Or are they just using you for their convenience.

We often have a hard time saying 'NO' to people because we don't want to upset them. Many of us tend to be people pleasers and that includes me at one point and this habit is very detrimental to our lives as I come to realize it a bit late. If someone truly needs help and you have the means and skills to do it. Of course , you should help them out as a kind gesture.

However, from my own experiences and what I observed in general. Most of the favors asked are for the asker's own convenience and help is not truly needed. So, you must decide for yourself if this person deserves your time. Remember, time is your life and time that you will never get back. **So, spend it wisely and offer it to those who truly deserve it.**

Ways to Get Some Extra Time

To squeeze more time out of the day, have you considered doing the following?

Are there tasks or chores you can hire someone to do for less than it costs you because your time is valuable, whereas you can use your time elsewhere to earn more money or do more important things?

Instead of listening to music while driving, how about listening to an audio book or educational podcast if you have a long commute.

While doing dishes or chores around the house, you can use this time to listen to an audio book or educational podcast too. I often do that myself.

Do you pick your clothes to wear the day before? Especially work clothes. It will save you a lot of time in the morning and not feel rushed for time. It also helps to avoid wearing mismatched socks or backward clothes to the office because you fumble in the dark. I have seen and heard many stories of mismatch wardrobes in the office. Don't be that person.

Do you put things back where they belong after use? Putting things back where they belong helps keep things organized and save time later when you need to use extra time and effort to organize and put them back again.

How about when you're waiting in line, rather it's in the grocery stores or coffee shops. You can use this time to micro read something interesting on your phone, or catch up on your emails, etc.

If you take the train or bus to work, you can make use of this time too, to do some reading, catch up on emails or do some work instead of listening to music or just looking out of the windows.

Do you plan and prepare your meals for the week? You can buy the necessary ingredients and things needed at the same time instead of making several trips to the grocery store.

When it comes to bills, do you set up auto payments? This is a huge time saver and not to mention avoid paying late fees if you forget to pay on time. We all have busy lives and often are forgetful. Having auto payments setup saves time and avoids paying late fees. Those late fees can add up. They can range from $25 to $50 or more.

Lastly, you might not think this tip is related to time saving but I am telling you it is. Have you ever had plans with friends or a meeting that was made a week ago, and they failed to show up because they forgot about it or remember the wrong day or time? Or sometimes things come up and they fail to let you know. Many people are inconsiderate of your time.

This tip is to save yourself from frustration and avoid wasting time. On the day of a meeting or gathering, if you know someone tends to have a forgetful tendency, give him or her a text to confirm the meeting/gathering place and time. I know you might say I shouldn't have to do that. We agreed on the place and time, and they should remember but often people are forgetful. You don't want to show up to a place only to find out they forgot about it. It only wastes your time. It happens more often than you think. Taking an extra minute to do that will save you time and disappointments.

Chapter 5

Examine Your Habits

We all have good habits and bad habits. A habit is defined as an action or behavior that we do repeatedly. Good habits are behaviors or actions that support your overall well-being, either emotionally, mentally, physically, or spiritually. Bad habits, on the other hand, are behaviors or actions that have a detrimental effect on your well-being.

Establishing good habits is essential for a person's well-being. However, good habits are a lot harder to form than bad ones. Good habits take conscious effort, it requires willpower, discipline, mental energy, persistence, and patience, etc. Bad habits are easier to form in nature because they don't require much effort.

If we all know that bad habits are detrimental to our well-being, why do we keep doing it? It is because our brains are wired to seek rewards or instant gratification or pleasure (dopamine seeking) which lead to bad habits such as addictions, compulsive or other unsupportive behaviors (Jeffrey, 2025).

Wouldn't you like to have more good habits and less of the bad habits? Sure, we all do but sometimes habits are hard to change or break. Your habits form your life, rather they are good or bad. To transform your life in a more positive direction, take an inventory of your daily habits and identify any bad habits that you wanted to remove or change. Our environment greatly influences our behavior.

For example, you are among a group of your teenage friends, who have all started smoking, due to peer pressure you will most likely pick up their smoking behavior even though you know that's bad for you. Peer pressure is a powerful influence on our habits and behaviors. Most of the time, people pick up a bad habit to mask their pain or temporarily numb their feelings or forget about their problems. Excessive drinking and doing drugs are two examples of coping mechanisms people use.

To form a new habit, it usually takes about 30 days of consistently working at it to stick. Good habits are best done slowly over a period with persistence and deliberate intention. We can't expect it to be changed or transformed overnight. It requires daily repetition. To help reduce resistance to change, starting by making small, incremental changes, it helps build momentum.

So how do we form more of the good habits? Do your current habits support your dreams and goals? Are they helping or hurting your well-being? As mentioned earlier, forming good habits takes effort and willpower. Let's examine the various habits one can develop in each category.

Physical Health Habits

- Exercise for at least 15 to 30 minutes
- Eating a healthy diet
- Have good posture
- Good hygiene
- Regular health checkups
- Cold showers
- Dress sharp /clean image

Mental and Emotional Health Habits

- Meditate daily
- Practice mindfulness
- Reduce screen time
- Daily journaling
- Doing brain exercises
- Reduce stress
- Self-reflect for areas of improvement
- Pay attention to your emotional triggers
- Positive self-talks
- Smile and laugh more often

Self–Development Habits

- Read uplifting, useful, or self-development books
- Learn new skills
- Setting goals and making plans to achieve it
- Attend self-development or skill enhancing seminars
- Watch self-development or useful videos

Financial Habits

- Save regularly
- Have retirement plans
- Investments
- Budgeting
- Examine spending habits
- Paying bills on time to avoid late fees

Relationships Habits

- Good communication skills
- Listening skills
- Spend quality time with loved ones
- Cultivate empathy

Spiritual Habits

- Practice forgiveness
- Gratitude journal
- Self- love
- Improve self-esteem
- Express yourself
- Spread kindness

Besides the above-mentioned habits, your environment has an impact on your habits as well. Such as having a clean and tidy home. Making sure everything is in an orderly fashion, and things are clean, helps reduce mental clutter and stress. The bedroom should be clean and calm, so distractions such as TVs or other devices should not be there. Also, limiting time spent on social media platforms is another good habit to form.

We mentioned some of the positive habits people can adopt in the above. What about some of the bad habits that people should try to change to improve their well-being? What is considered a bad habit? A bad habit is a habit that has a detrimental effect on your well-being.

The following are generally considered as bad habits: Smoking, doing drugs, excess drinking, gambling, porn, gossiping, complaining, criticizing, overeating, bad posture, always late to meetings or gatherings, people pleasing or inability to say no, etc.

These are just a sample of bad habits that people might have. We all know to some extent that these habits don't serve us well, but we still do it. But why?

As mentioned before, bad habits are easy to form. We might have developed these habits growing up, due to the environment we are in, simply as an escape mechanism from our problems and difficulties we face in life.

So, how do we break bad habits? First, that person has to make the decision that he/she wants to break this habit and to make a change. Without this first step, it simply won't work.

Any habit change requires willpower, dedication, and persistence to make it effective. For example, someone decides that he wants to quit smoking. In his mind, he has to be mentally prepared for it. Every time a craving for a cigarette appears, he has to mentally control his cravings or use a substitute to distract his mind like chewing gum or some other substitute. It won't be easy at first and probably relapses the first few times but if he keeps at it and each time prolongs the cravings further and further, pretty soon his craving tendency will reduce over time, and he no longer has the urge to smoke after a period of time.

Again, any changes require time, willpower, and persistence. The key is to start small and make incremental changes over time, and it will become a lot easier as time goes on.

Our habits are the building blocks of our lives. Practicing good habits increases our well-being, mentally and physically. Be aware of your habits and make any necessary changes. Ask yourself, does this habit support my dreams and goals in life? Does it help me physically or mentally in any way? If not, maybe it's time to make a change.

Chapter 6

Invest In Yourself

In today's competitive world, your job or career can be taken away at any moment. Think of the recent waves of layoffs in various sectors from tech to retail in the years 2023 - 2024. However, the skills and knowledge you acquired can never be taken away from you. With the skills and the experiences you possess, you can always find a new or better job. As long as you have the skills and knowledge, you can always find ways to make a living or start your own business. That's why it's so important to invest in yourself.

What do we mean when we say invest in yourself and how do we invest in ourselves? Investing in ourselves requires us to have a life-learning mindset. Here are some ways and methods to invest in ourselves.

Reading Books Daily

Reading is the best way to increase your knowledge and expose yourselves to or acquire new ideas. There are books on all subjects you can think of to read upon. Reading expands our horizon and takes us to a magical or fascinating place that we can't dream of ourselves.

Reading improves our focus and concentration. It improves our memories and mentally stimulates us. It helps build up vocabulary and improve our writing skills. It also has a calming effect and helps reduce stress. These are just some of the many benefits of reading daily.

Learn Something New Every Day

Everyday try to learn something or do something new. For example, learn a new vocabulary, pick up a new hobby, take a different but safe route to work so we can be exposed to different surroundings or discover new things, or explore new ways of doing something, etc.

Acquiring New Skills or Knowledge

The best way to acquire new skills or knowledge besides reading books is attending seminars, workshops, classes or watching educational videos. Make every effort to attend as many educational seminars as you can. These days, there are many educational videos readily available on the internet, which you can fit into your schedule easily.

Improve Your Communication Skills

It's vital to be able to express ourselves clearly in business and personal settings. The ability to express our ideas and thoughts in clear and concise ways is an invaluable skill. To improve our communication skills, we have to build up our vocabulary library and practice speaking in public and joining speaking groups such as Toastmasters International.

Learning to be a better listener is part of good communication. When you listen to what the other person is saying, you can respond appropriately and not in an incoherent way that has nothing to do with what they are saying. It also shows that you're paying attention and makes the speaker feel heard. It builds rapport and fosters better connections between each other.

Challenge Yourself

Challenge yourself to grow and do something outside of your comfort zone. By stepping outside of your comfort zone, you can learn more about yourself, your abilities and discover that you are more capable than you think.

For example, you have been wanting to do more traveling but sometimes find it hard to coordinate time or schedule with family or friends. The places that you wanted to go might not be of interest to them or that they don't have the means to do it. You have not done any international travel on your own before. Now you're thinking of travelling on your own but worry about things such as personal safety, a possible feeling of loneliness, not being able to share the experience or the cost.

Some ways to help overcome these concerns might be to start taking local trips such as nearby cities or states on your own to see how you feel. Joining tour groups is a great way to travel, you are on your own yet not really. You can meet fellow travelers in the group, so you won't feel like you're by yourself. From what I read, staying in hostels is also a good way to meet other travelers.

Some important keys to solo travel are to do your research beforehand, pick a destination that is inherently safer, know where to go and where not to go. Have emergency plans. Millions of people all over the world have done it, so can you.

Expand Your Network

We all have heard of the term "Your network is your net worth". The people around you have a huge impact on your life. So, choose the people around you wisely, choose people who uplift and inspire you. You can learn from people who are more experienced, work in a different field or industry, or generally more knowledgeable.

You can learn from their mistakes and be exposed to different environments, ideas, ways of thinking which you might not have thought of before. Limit your time with people who are negative such as complainers, gossipers, or people who have no desire to better themselves but yet constantly complain.

Develop and Practice Self-Discipline

In order to get things done, we need to have self-discipline. Many times, we will face difficulties or roadblocks in completing a task or achieving a goal. Without self-discipline, we will procrastinate or simply give up when we encounter difficulties.

Self-discipline is doing the hard work even if we don't want to or feel like it. Self-discipline is defined as "the ability to control one's impulses, emotions, and behaviors in order to achieve long-term goals" (Murphy, 2024). Self-discipline is delaying immediate gratifications and has a long-term view mindset. So, developing self-discipline is crucial for achieving your goals and well-being.

Chapter 7

Raise Your Self-Esteem and Self-Confidence

No matter if you're rich or poor, we all deal with issues such as lack of self-confidence and self-esteem to some degree. Having a healthy dose of self-esteem and self-confidence greatly increases the quality of your life. On the other hand, if you are lacking in these areas, it's very detrimental to your overall well-being.

The environment we grew up in and the people we surround ourselves with have a tremendous impact on our lives. They have the power to influence how we feel and think of ourselves such as our self-esteem and self-confidence. Our past experiences also shaped who we are today and how we view the world.

Self-Confidence vs Self-Esteem

Many people use the term self-confidence and self-esteem interchangeably and often confuse them as being the same thing. However, these two terms are distinctively different from one another and refer to different elements of our behaviors and characteristics (Explore Psychology, 2024).

Self-confidence is defined as your belief in your ability to handle specific tasks or situations. Your confidence can vary greatly depending on your level of skills, ability, or knowledge of the topic or subject.

Self-esteem is defined as your overall sense of self-worth or how you view yourself as a person regardless of outside factors or influences. Self-esteem can be viewed as your internal foundation that stays relatively stable. However, they may change over time based on your experiences or personal growth journey.

Let's explore these two terms in greater details below:

Self-Confidence

What is self-confidence? Self-confidence is when you hold a belief that you have the ability to accomplish a task or handle a specific situation. This belief comes from your past experiences, skills or knowledge you possess, or through repeated practices.

For example, you have to give a presentation in front of a large audience. On the day of your presentation, you feel very confident that you will do well because you have been practicing your speech and going over your materials every day for the past week. Through your daily practices, your self-confidence grew because your belief in yourself grew.

Many people lack self-confidence because they don't believe in themselves and their abilities. If you're lacking in this area and want to increase your self-confidence, what are some things you can do to increase your self-confidence?

Below are some ways one can increase one's self-confidence:

- Increase your knowledge
- Build skills
- Practice daily
- Try new things or take up new hobbies
- Break-down task into smaller parts
- Always learning something new
- Research and plan ahead
- Believe in yourself and your abilities

Do things or activities that bring you joy and happiness. Such as taking up a hobby, learning salsa dancing, journaling, learning photography or fly a drone. Learn a new skill such as cooking Italian food or a new foreign language, making video contents, etc.

Harness the lessons learned to improve your future decision-making skills. The lessons we learned from past experiences help us grow as a person and enhance our self-developments.

Keep a Journal of Your Accomplishments and Good Qualities You Possess

Often, people forget how capable they are and all the things that they have accomplished in their lifetime.

Another way to boost your self-confidence is to list all the good qualities about you and your accomplishments. You might say that you don't have many, but you do.

For example, list all the good qualities about you such as: compassionate, courageous, dependable, disciplined, helpful, humorous, innovative, joyful, kind, loyal, responsible, self-disciplined, trustworthy, etc.

Sometimes we forget how accomplished we are because we don't view them as accomplishments. Such as when we graduated from college and landed our first job. Or when we save up enough money to buy big ticket items such as a car or house. You volunteer at various charities and help someone in need, etc.

How about things such as completing a hard project at work, running a marathon, traveling by yourself, or move to another state or country from family and now you have to be self-reliant, etc. All these things take courage or skills. Keeping a journal of all these qualities and accomplishments no matter how small it seems to remind yourself from time to time of your qualities and the abilities you possess and that you have the capability to accomplish great things.

Self-Esteem

Self-esteem on the other hand is all about how you view your self-worth. It is an internal view of oneself and the internal dialogue and self-talk.

The root of our self-esteem is from our childhood and our upbringing. It is based on our early life experiences and the people around us. For example, if you grow up in a household that lacks love and support. You will feel that you're not good enough to receive good things or a belief that you don't deserve good things in life such as love, happiness, and success, etc.

When people have a low self-esteem, they tend to seek approval from others and put others' needs before themselves because they view their needs as not as important. This behavior of always trying to please others or put other people on the pedestal often leads to people taking advantage of them or being an easy target for bullying because the bully knows they will not stand up for themselves.

A low self-esteem person often has a hard time saying "NO" for the fear of offending the other person or letting people cross their boundaries.

Oftentimes, people don't realize that they have a low self-esteem, or the boundaries have crossed because of the environment they grew up in or just how they were brought up.

For example, if you were brought up in an environment where you were told to be a good person, you have to always help people regardless of whether they deserve it or not or you live a sheltered life where everyone is good to you, and you assume others in the outside world will not take advantage of you.

Unfortunately, in the real world, just because you are good to them doesn't mean they will be good to you. Yes, we should help people if they truly need our help but often people are just taking advantage of your kindness. They don't really need help but for their own convenience or selfish reasons. It's important to recognize when or who to give your time and energy to. Not everyone deserves your time or resources.

So, how can we increase or boost our self-esteem? I would say the number one thing is knowing your self-worth. You deserve all the good things that life has to offer just as everyone else.

Learning to say **"no"** to things or situations that you don't want to participate in or align with your goals or bring value to your life without feeling guilty or fear of being judged. This will take practice and will not change overnight but keep at it and you will see how your life will be transformed in a positive way.

A low self-esteem person often lets other people cross their boundaries. When you don't say anything when someone crosses your boundaries, they will think you are ok with the way they treat you.

It's very important to set boundaries of what behaviors or actions you will not tolerate. When you set boundaries, you let people know you will not accept bad behaviors or mistreatment. Don't be afraid to end the relationship if necessary in order to protect your well-being. Remember, you don't need someone who mistreats you.

Be kind to yourself. Oftentimes, we show kindness and forgiveness to others but are very critical of ourselves for every little thing. Be self-aware and replace any negative thoughts with positive ones. Remember, you are human also and have flaws just like others. We are worthy of love, happiness and success for just being ourselves. Always remember you are a worthy and valuable human being regardless of external factors.

Self-confidence and self-esteem go hand in hand. They are interrelated. When you have more self-confidence, you have more self-esteem and likewise.

Having a healthy dose of both can greatly improve your well-being and be better equipped to handle life's situations and challenges.

If you want to boost your self-esteem and self-confidence, practice the ideas and strategies mentioned above and you will see the positive effects they have on your life. You're deserving of all the good things life has to offer.

Chapter 8

People and Relationships

PEOPLE

Ah, PEOPLE. This is one of the many things that I wish I had learned earlier, which is how to recognize early on the different types of potentially toxic people and how to handle them. The people you let into your life can be a blessing or a curse. Learning to recognize toxic traits or behaviors early on can save you from stress, drama, your overall well-being, and even the harm they might bring to you.

As human beings, we interact and socialize and encounter all types of people in our daily lives. All people have negative and positive traits. However, there are some people who tend to have more negative traits than positive ones.

Have you ever spent time with someone who just drains your energy or puts you in a bad mood whenever you spend time with them? They tend to complain about everything and have a lot of drama in their lives. They always put the blame on others and never examine themselves as part of their problems. They don't like their situation, yet they never put any effort or time into taking necessary steps or actions to correct their issues or problems. It's exhausting to listen to their constant complaints.

When we first meet someone new, we don't really know much about them. Most of the time, we are not consciously thinking rather this person will have a positive or negative effect on our lives. We are just getting to know them. We all tend to put on our best behaviors or best front initially and in the early stage of the encounters.

However, as we spend more time or socialize with the person, if we pay close attention, we will see certain traits or behaviors about this person. There are red flags and telltale signs that this person could be a toxic person or potential to bring drama into your life. Yet often we ignore or brush these warning signs aside.

If you don't learn to recognize these traits or signs, and take actions to limit the interaction, before you know it, they are deeply embedded in your life and now it's much harder to disconnect from them. Rather they're just acquaintances, friends, romantic partners, or other people you might encounter; these are some of the early red flags you might want to look for.

For example, if this person you just recently met and barely knew them. They already have a list of favors that they are asking you to do for them. This person is not interested in developing a meaningful, mutually beneficial connection. They are more interested in what they can get out of you.

Another example along the same line as above is, when someone constantly asks you for favors but would not do the same if you ask. These types of people will only take from you but will never give in return. I am not saying you should expect favors returned whenever you do something, what I am saying is, if you ever need a favor, they should be able to return one if it's within their ability. Recognizing this is a one-way relationship early on can help you stop being taken advantage of and give your time and resources to someone who truly deserves it where the relationship is mutually beneficial.

Most of the time people ask for favors for their own convenience and not because they truly need help. We all have a limited amount of time in the day, by choosing to give our time to people who truly need it, this makes our time worthwhile and well spent. Also, we don't want to help them develop the bad habit of dependency and not taking responsibility for their own lives.

Of course, if someone truly needs our help and we have the capability or resources to do so, we should definitely lend a helping hand whenever possible.

Other types of people you should limit your time with or toxic behaviors to be on the lookout for are:

Narcissist

A narcissist is someone who possesses narcissistic behaviors such as they tend to disregard others' feelings, they have a sense of entitlement and self-importance, use manipulative behaviors, need for admiration, lack of empathy, and display arrogance, etc. These types of people will only think about themselves (WebMD Editorial, 2023).

Manipulators

Manipulators use tactics and behaviors to influence or obtain power and control over someone (Ibe, 2023). They use tactics such as exploiting your weakness for personal gain. They gaslight you when you confront them with an issue and make it seem like it's your fault. They use guilt as a weapon against you such as making you feel guilty when you refuse to do what they want. They criticize you or make you feel insecure with the purpose of eroding your self-confidence, etc.

These are a few examples of tactics of manipulators. By recognizing these signs and tactics, you can be better equipped to protect yourself such as calling them out for their behaviors or limiting your exposure to them to ensure your well-being.

People Who Gossip

When someone talks badly about another person in front of you. You can bet this person talks badly about you to another person too. These kinds of people like to get into other people's personal lives and love to spread misinformation. Most of the time the information they get is from second or third-hand knowledge.

Complainer

Another type of person you should limit your time with are people who constantly complain about things or situations, yet they never take steps or actions to correct them. It's always someone else's fault or they have some excuses as to why they are in the situation. It's exhausting to be around constant complainers, and it also negatively affects your mental well-being.

Always Taker, Never Giver

Relationships and connections should be mutually beneficial. When the relationship is balanced, both lives are enhanced because of it. However, when it's one-sided where one only takes from but never gives, then this relationship is problematic and causes us to have a not so good feeling about this relationship or even a sense of being taken advantage of.

Always Drama

There are certain people who always seem to attract drama into their lives. To protect your mental well-being, avoid being sucked into their drama.

Jealousy and Envy

As human beings, we all have some degrees of jealousy and envy. However, beware of the type of people who make you feel guilty or bad about your success or accomplishment and make it seem like you don't deserve it or try to make you feel bad about it.

What these people don't realize is the amount of dedication and time you spend to accomplish them. Some people even accuse you of making them look bad because of their own failings. How absurd, right? We are all responsible for our own lives and the choices we make.

Learning to recognize these types of behaviors or traits, you're better equipped to stand up for yourself if someone tries to put you down or makes you feel bad or guilty. I am not saying all people are bad, just some. As a matter of fact, there are a lot of good people out there, but we can't ignore that there are bad apples amongst them.

We also have to be mindful that lots of people who behave badly or have bad traits could be due to their upbringing, childhood traumas, or bad environment they are in, thus, giving them some grace but at the same time, we need to protect our well-being by limiting our exposure and potential negative effects from them.

Take an inventory of the people who are currently in your life. Ask yourself how this person is impacting your life? Are they mostly a positive force or a negative one? How important is this person in your life? Do you give away your time and resources easily to people without considering if they truly deserve it?

From what I see and my own experience, we tend to do the MOST for the LEAST deserving people. Why? Because, we have this tendency to be people-pleasing. These undeserving people are never satisfied or feel that you're not doing enough, so you keep doing or giving to gain their approval, UNTIL one day you wake up and realized, wait the minute, **why am I doing so much for this person when they haven't done a damn thing for me,** not only that, but they also don't show appreciation or gratefulness in what you're doing for them.

Most of the time they're not even important people in our life yet we give them the most to please them because for whatever reason we don't want to offend them somehow. I know, humans are irrational.

So, learn to be selective in how you give your time and resources and **learn to say "NO"** to anything that doesn't align with your values or have a positive impact on your life. Your time is valuable, only give to those who truly deserve it.

RELATIONSHIPS

During our lifetime, we will form many types of relationships such as work-related, friendship, romantic relationships, and family relationships. Having good harmonious relationships makes our life more meaningful and enjoyable.

Learning to navigate these relationships can be challenging at times. After all, as human beings, we all have different traits and personalities. What works for one person might not be for another person.

Let's examine the various relationship dynamics.

Work-Relationships

At work, we have to interact with various departmental staffs and work together in order to get the work done. Because your co-workers are human beings, they will have different personalities. Some of the things one can do to make the workplace more harmonious are, be courteous, be mindful of other people's time, lend a helping hand when needed, be a team player, and show appreciation, etc.

When conflicts arise, learn how to resolve them amicably. Give praise when it's deserving to encourage good performance.

Friendships

Your friendship circle has a great impact on your life. There's a famous saying that goes "You're the average of the five people you spend the most time with", so choose your friends wisely. Having good friends enriches our lives and expands our experiences. We spend a great deal of time with friends doing various things and activities. A good friendship is mutually beneficial and has a positive impact on our well-being.

Good friends can be a source of support when you need them. Although they can be a source of support, you shouldn't dump your problems onto them and expect them to solve them for you without you taking actions or making necessary changes.

The characteristics of a good friend are they look after you and have your best interest. They stand up for you and never do or say things to put you down. They don't gossip behind your back. **They don't try to take advantage of you. They treat you fairly and don't overstep your boundaries. The relationship is balanced and you both benefit mutually.** If they don't possess these qualities, put them in the acquaintances category, not good friends. Of course, you should try to set an example of a good friend too.

Romantic-Relationships

When it comes to romantic relationships, I am the last person you should take advice from as I am so bad at it. Take this section with a "grain of salt". However, I did learn a few lessons and recognize some common mistakes like most people encounter in their love-relationships.

A romantic relationship can put you on **cloud nine** or a **nightmare** on Elm Street. We all wish for a long-lasting romantic relationship that leads to marriage and becoming life-long partners. Yet, many relationships don't last for more than 5 years. Romantic relationships tend to come and go for various reasons, rather it's incompatibility in values or goals, different stages in life, financial reasons, commitment issues, lack of communications & trust, or infidelity, etc.

Nowadays, with so many dating apps available, dating becomes even harder for people to commit and put in the time & effort to get to know someone because they can easily match with so many people. This creates the tendency to always look for the next best thing or so they think.

When it comes to dating, we seem to always attract the same type of people. Why is that? It is because we like familiarity. We are more comfortable with things or situations that we have encountered before, people in general don't like changes. We like to stay in our comfort zone.

So how can we break this pattern? First, examine why the relationship didn't work out. What are some of the issues that your relationship encounters? Are they situation based? Such as like where they live (distance), different stage in life (career focused), or financial related, etc., or are they have to do with the person itself, such as certain bad behaviors, etc.?

Have you ever thought about what your ideal partner looks like, such as having certain qualities that you look for? Oftentimes, we get into a relationship because it just happened, or they happened to appear in the right place, but we are not consciously choosing them based on the qualities that we are actually looking for. After dating them for a while, you realize they are not quite what you're looking for. Therefore, you don't feel happy or have that feeling that something is missing.

When we feel unsatisfied or frustrated, then the relationship starts to crack. If the issues are not resolved, that's when people start to look around, cheat, or end the relationship. Oftentimes, romantic-relationship require the willingness to compromise, without it, most will not succeed.

Whenever we get into a relationship, especially the long-term ones, we invest time, resources and most importantly, emotion into that person and open up to the possibility of being hurt. I wish there's an **on/off** button to our emotions, because breakups can be devastating to experience. Luckily, we usually get over it over time, and hopefully we learn something from the experience, and avoid the same mistakes next time.

So how can we make better decisions in picking partners? There is no magic formula that will guarantee success. However, there're a few things we can do to increase the chances of long-term success.

Have a clear idea of what you want, know your deal breakers, ask lots of important questions in the very beginning to see if your goals and lifestyle **align** with each other, have good communications, don't stay in a dead-end or toxic relationship because you're afraid of being on your own.

The longer you stay in a wrong relationship, you waste time and opportunity in finding the relationship that's better for you. Time is especially important for women who want to have children. So often people stay in a relationship hoping for changes to happen, and before you know it, many years have gone by, and when the relationship finally ends, by then, you have put yourself behind the 8th ball especially for women in the older age group.

A good romantic relationship can enhance our lives and add to our overall well-being. However, not everyone is so lucky, some romantic-relationships not only don't add to our well-being, but they can bring stress, chaos, drama, or even harm (violence, drugs, abuse, etc.) into your life. So, choose your partners wisely and date with intention if long-term is what you're looking for.

Family-Relationships

Family is the most important thing to us next to our health. Our family is the center of our universe. It brings us joy and gives us meaning to life. Our family is the reason we work hard to have a better life. I am lucky to have a great family and maintain a good relationship with all my family members. I love spending quality time with my family and celebrating holidays together. Those are the best feelings; it warms my heart and makes me happy whenever we get together.

Unfortunately, not all people have good relationships with their family members due to various reasons. It makes me sad when I hear about people who don't get along with their children, siblings, or parents. They are the closest people in our lifetime. Whatever the conflicts are between you and them, we should find a way to resolve them and repair the relationships before it's too late.

Sometimes, we think our loved ones will be here forever, even though we all know in the back of our mind that's not the case. It just is not something we think about or be conscious of that fact. We are all too busy trying to make a living or living a busy life where we don't slow down to ponder what's truly important in our lives.

If you haven't talked to your loved one for a while, please give them a call and remind them how important they are to you. If you need to repair or forgive someone, please do it now when you have a chance to repair the relationship.

Our family members are the most important thing to us, we should cherish the time we have with them because we all know they won't be here forever. Slow down and cherish the quality time you have with loved ones. They give us meanings in life. So, cherish them.

PART TWO

SMART INVESTMENTS

Chapter 9

Examine Your Current Financial Health

What happens if one day, you wake up and see your bank account showing a balance of $1,000,000. This amount might not seem to be a big deal for many entrepreneurs or businesspeople. It is a big deal for most of the average working people.

We all dreamed of becoming a millionaire or being financially independent, not because we love money, ok, maybe a little bit of that, but rather the idea of what money can do for us, such as the freedom to choose how we spend our time, to provide our family with a better quality of life, or buy that dream home, etc.

You might wonder, how did some people become millionaires or even billionaires? One thing is for sure, it's not from a 9 to 5 job unless you're the CEO of a major corporation. Sure, some people are lucky and become multi-millionaires or billionaires because they're born into rich families such as if you're children or other members of the Rockefeller family. However, even with the Rockefellers, they didn't make their fortunes overnight.

The Rockefellers brothers, John D. Rockefeller and William D. Rockefeller are business entrepreneurs. They made their fortunes mainly from the petroleum industry and other business ventures in the 19th and early 20th centuries (Wikipedia, 2024). You can say that the Rockefeller brothers are self-made billionaires because of their business ventures. The same is true for many other business entrepreneurs around the world who made a fortune from their businesses.

As you can see, having a business is one of the ways many people acquire their fortunes. However, not many people have the resources or skills to become an entrepreneur. So, what other ways can someone increase their fortune or become more financially well off? One method is through investing, another is learning how to keep more of the money you have.

Let's take a look at your current financial situation. Where does your money come from (income) and where is it going to (expenses)? Does your income only briefly stay in your account and then you have to use it immediately to pay for expenses such as your rent, insurance, food, and other basic living expenses without much left afterwards?

How are you spending your money? Do you buy things that you don't actually need but want to follow a trend or need to have the latest or greatest things constantly. We love to do impulse buying, and afterwards we change our mind or realize that we don't really like it as much as we initially thought. One way to counter impulse buying is to pause and give it time such as waiting at least 24 hours to see if you still want it. Do you buy the same type of clothes or things, even if you already own like 10 of them?

For example, as a female, we all love to have a couple nice black dresses in our wardrobe. But if you already own like 10 of them in similar style, do you really need another one? I am guilty of this habit too; many dresses or clothes are still sitting in my closet with tags. Do you buy things that lose value once they're out the door? Have you done an analysis of where most of your money is going? How about savings, do you set aside a percentage of your income in savings or for investing?

Your money habits have a lot to do with your current financial situation. Because we live in a credit-based society (i.e. credit cards), it's easy to swipe that plastic card and buy things without considering that we have to pay it back later. Since we don't hand the store the physical money when we buy things, we don't really feel the true cost of it.

The average American are heavily in debt in their credit spendings. Majority of credit cards have an interest rate of 20 % to 25% or more applied to their balances. Each month, most of the people are making the bare minimum required repayment or worse not paying at all. Thus, those interest or late fees are added to their balance and making it harder and longer to pay off that balance.

How many sources of income do you have? Is your income mostly from your 9 to 5 day job? And perhaps, some from your 401k or Pension? You see; in order to build wealth, you need to use the money you have to make more of it. You can only work a certain number of hours a day; most rich people have many sources of income and are making money even while in their sleep. It's called passive income.

Passive income is defined as money that is not earned through a traditional job where you have to do work like your 9 to 5 job which is based on the hours you worked. Passive income requires little or no work from you and it's not dependent on the number of hours you put in. Examples of passive income are such as rental income, investment income, etc.

Let's examine the strategies to employ to increase your wealth and the types of passive income and investments available in the following chapters.

Chapter 10

Build Wealth with Real Estates

Have you ever heard of the saying "The rich are getting richer"? That's because the rich understood the game of money and use it to their advantage. They don't let their money sit around. They use their money to make more of it through various investment vehicles and employ careful tax planning and strategies to keep more of it.

If you want to be more financially independent, you too can employ some of these same strategies. Let's look at some of the investment vehicles and strategies available.

Real Estates

If you ask, what industry produces the most millionaires or billionaires? You will find that the majority of them are involved in the real estate industry in some shape or form. Most of the Multi-millionaires own a large portfolio of real estates all around the world.

Why? Because real estate in general holds value and appreciates in value over time and it's a more stable investment compared to other types. What are some ways to generate wealth through real estate?

Buy Real Estate as Primary Home

Since real estate values appreciate over time, buying and holding the real estate for a period of time and selling it later for a higher value is one way to add to your wealth.

Nowadays, you can put as little as 3% down payment. The first step is figuring out how much of a house you can afford, and the monthly payment required. Keep in mind there are other costs that are associated with owning a house, such as property taxes, insurance, maintenance, etc. Can you afford the monthly payment after all your expenses?

Owning your own home builds equity. How much rent are you currently paying compared to your monthly payment if you were to buy a property. Say if you're currently paying $1,500 a month for rent compared to the mortgage payment of $1,400 after the

3% down payment. Essentially, you can use that rent money to pay yourself and build equity.

Another advantage of owning your own primary home is tax savings. When you decide to sell your home, you can exclude up to $250,000 for single filers or $500,000 for married couples, of capital gain from the sale of your primary residence according to the IRS. For example, you and your husband bought a home as your primary residence 10 years ago for $150,000. Now, both of you have decided to sell it and the house is sold for $500,000. You will have a capital gain of $350,000 ($500,000 - $150,000 = $350,000). Since this is your primary residence, you can exclude up to $500,000 as a married couple, essentially the $350,000 gain is tax free.

However, in order to qualify for this exclusion (Section 121 exclusion), you must meet both the ownership test and the use test. You must own and occupy your home for the last 2 of the 5 years prior to the sale date. For more detailed information, please visit the IRS website for Publication 523 and Section 121 exclusion rules.

Buy Real Estate for Rental Income

Many people buy real estate property to rent out to others to generate rental income. Rental income is considered passive income because it requires little time from you once you have your tenant in place. Of course, occasionally, it might still require your attention such as maintenance work, making sure tenants pay rent on time, keeping the property in working order, etc.

Rental property also comes with tax benefits in the form of deductions. You can deduct things such as property tax, insurance, depreciation, maintenance and repair costs, and many other things that are associated with your rental property. For more detailed information about what you can deduct, please visit the IRS website.

Flipping Houses (properties)

Real estate properties generally take a while to appreciate value. Depending on the location and market conditions it can take many years to see a substantial increase in value.

Some real estate investors might not want to wait that long to see a return on their investment.

Thus, they choose house flipping as a strategy to shorten the time required to generate return on investment. House flipping is the process of buying a property at a lower price (usually a fixer-upper property) and fixing it up (remodel it) and then putting it on the market for sale for a higher price to generate a profit. This process usually takes about 3 to 6 months from the time of purchase to sale of the property. Sometimes, it might take a little longer but usually it's under a year.

House flipping is not for everyone, many skills are required of you. It's vital to know your market and choose the right location and the types and conditions of the properties suitable for flipping. Before considering any property for flipping, you need to do an analysis of the current condition of the house and how much is required to remodel it.

You need to know the zoning laws and permits needed. You need to have experience dealing and negotiating with contractors. You need to make sure to pick reputable contractors who are reliable and do quality work. Hiring the wrong contractors can delay putting the property in the market or worse cost you a lot of money to correct their mistakes.

Flipping houses can be a quick way to make a profit. For example, you find a decent fixer-upper that costs you around $105,000 but you know the houses in the area are selling for $300,000 or more. You think you can bring the house to good condition for around $65,000. If you sold the property for around $310,000. You would have made a profit of $140,000 = [$310,000 − ($105,000+$65,000)] in a relatively short period of time.

Although flipping properties can be a good way to generate income, there are many things to consider, and a different skill set is required and it's more complicated. It's not as easy as just fixing a property and selling it for a higher price. There are lots of conditions and things to consider. For example, are you able to find a buyer for the price target you plan to sell it at? Do you have the capital for renovation and remodeling costs? Flipping property usually requires a lot more capital upfront.

Do you know how to pick a good location for flipping? For example, you shouldn't put so much money into renovating and creating a million-dollar home in an area that usually doesn't sell for more than $500,000. Likewise, you don't want to convert a two-flat property to a nice big single-family home and hope to sell it for $750,000, when the single-family home in that area is selling no more than $450,000.

I have seen some investors who did that without understanding the area. In that area, no one is willing to pay that kind of price for a single-family home. That property has been sitting in the market for over a year, not sure if it ever got sold, I lost track of it. If it did, I am pretty sure it's substantially less than the $750,000 asking price.

Flipping property can be complicated and it's not for everyone. However, it can be a strategy one can employ if you have the skills and resources to do it well.

Chapter 11

The Hidden Power of IRAs

Types of IRAs

Many people look forward to their retirement where they don't have to work at their 9 to 5 jobs anymore and have the money to go travel or do whatever they want. With the main source of income stopped, most will be relying on the income from their Social Security, Pensions or IRAs.

IRA stands for an Individual Retirement Account. They are retirement accounts that the government has established rules and policies on. There are many types of IRAs available such as Traditional IRA, Roth IRA, Simple IRA, Self-Directed IRA, SEP IRA, etc.

401(k)s are also considered IRA accounts, the difference is that 401(k)s are offered through employers (thru your job) and some employers also match up to a certain % of your contribution amount.

In this book, I will mainly focus on these 3 types of IRAs, that is the Traditional IRA, Roth IRA and 401(k).

I wanted to talk about the general rules about IRAs. IRAs are retirement accounts. They are meant for providing supplemental income for retirees during retirement, if you withdraw money before you reach the age of 59 1/2, you might be subject to a 10% penalty. The 59 ½ age requirement applies to IRAs withdrawals, not to be confused with the age requirement for claiming Social Security benefits which can range from 62 for early retirement, and from 65 to 67 depending on when you were born.

If you withdraw before you reach the age of 59 ½, there's a 10% penalty. There are some exceptions where you can avoid the 10% penalty if you meet those exceptions. Also, the combined total contributions from all Traditional and Roth IRAs cannot be more the yearly contribution amount limit.

In the later sections, I will talk more about each type of IRAs in detail such as how much one can contribute each year, who can contribute, and the exceptions to the 10% withdrawal penalty rule, etc.

Roth IRA

Let's first start with "Roth IRA" because I think this is such a great retirement and investment vehicle that everyone should have a Roth IRA account in their investment portfolio.

A little history about how the Roth IRA came about, it was enacted in 1997 with the passage of the Taxpayer Relief Act of 1997. Roth IRA was originally called an "IRA Plus" and was proposed by Senator Bob Packwood of Oregon and Senator William Roth of Delaware. The Roth IRA is named after Senator William Roth. When the idea was first proposed in 1989, the plan was to allow individuals to invest up to $2,000 in an account with no immediate tax deduction, and the earnings are tax-free when withdrawn later at retirement (Kurt, 2024).

Essentially, all the money that grows inside the Roth IRA account will be tax-free if withdrawn after reaching age of 59 ½ and you held the account for 5 years or more.

How would you like to have $5 Billion Tax-Free money in your Roth IRA account? That's exactly what happened to Peter Thiel's Roth IRA account. You might or might not have heard about it, but it made the headlines over all the mainstream media such as NBC News (Farivar, 2021).

According to an article from NBC News, where they cited their source of their information from ProPublica, a nonprofit news organization, they said that ProPublica claimed to uncover a "vast trove of Internal Revenue Service data on the tax returns of thousands of the nation's wealthiest people, covering more than 15 years (Farivar, 2021)." NBC News said they couldn't reach ProPublica to verify this information.

According to ProPublica, the documents showed Peter Thiel, who is the co-founder of PayPal, that he started a Roth IRA in 1999 with just $2,000 at the time. Thiel had the idea of putting the startup's shares (PayPal) into a traditional IRA, but Tom Anderson, the adviser and retired president of PENSCO Trust Company advised Peter Thiel and other PayPal executives to put their early shares of the company into a Roth IRA instead.

According to ProPublica, "Thiel allegedly paid $0.0001 per share of PayPal and bought 1.7 million shares for $1,700. Three years later, in 2002, eBay acquired PayPal. Thiel sold his 1.7 million PayPal shares but kept all of the proceeds inside his Roth IRA account. By the end of that year, Thiel's Roth IRA was worth $28.5 million. In 2004, when Thiel spend $500,000 and received in return a substantive stake in Facebook (Farivar, 2021)."

As you can see, how powerful the Roth IRA can be as a wealth building tool. Most of us are unlikely to be able to grow our Roth IRA as much as Peter Thiel does because we don't have access to early startup shares. However, we can still grow our account substantially if we pick and invest in solid and reputable companies. All the gains inside this Roth IRA account will be tax-free if withdrawn when you reach the age of 59 ½ and have held the account for 5 years, then all the money inside this account is tax-free. Think about that.

Let's look at some rules and requirements of a Roth IRA.

As of this writing in the year 2024, the contribution limit for both Roth and Traditional IRA is $7,000 for those under 50 age and $8,000 for age 50 and older. Remember, the limit is a combined total for Roth and Traditional IRA. For example, if you're under 50 years old, you can contribute $3,000 to a Traditional IRA and $4,000 to a Roth IRA, but the total cannot be more than $7,000. Otherwise, you might have to pay a penalty on the excess amount if you contribute over the limit. Roth IRA contributions are not tax deductible. However, all the contributions and gains inside Roth IRA are tax-free when withdrawn at age 59 ½ and you meet all the requirements.

Anyone can contribute to a Roth IRA; however, you must have earned income to be able to contribute and you can't contribute more than your earned income. For example, in 2024, a student with an earned income of $6,000 through part-time work can only contribute up to $6,000 even though the limit is $7,000.

Also, there's an upper income limit as to who can contribute depending on your modified adjusted gross income (MAGI). Please see the table below.

This table shows whether your contribution to a Roth IRA is affected by the amount of your modified AGI as computed for Roth IRA purpose.

If your filing status is...	And your modified AGI is...	Then you can contribute...
married filing jointly or qualifying surviving spouse	< $230,000	up to the limit
married filing jointly or qualifying surviving spouse	≥ $230,000 but < $240,000	a reduced amount
married filing jointly or qualifying surviving spouse	≥ $240,000	zero
married filing separately and you lived with your spouse at any time during the year	< $10,000	a reduced amount
married filing separately and you lived with your spouse at any time during the year	≥ $10,000	zero
single, head of household, or married filing separately and you did not live with your spouse at any time during the year	< $146,000	up to the limit
single, head of household, or married filing separately and you did not live with your spouse at any time during the year	≥ $146,000 but < $161,000	a reduced amount
single, head of household, or married filing separately and you did not live with your spouse at any time during the year	≥ $161,000	zero

Source: www.irs.gov

Some things to remember about Roth IRA are that it's not deductible; but it's tax free when withdrawn after reaching the age of 59 1/2 and you meet all the requirements. There's no minimum distribution requirement. You can leave the amounts in your Roth IRA as long as you live.

One important thing regarding the Roth IRA is that you must hold your account for 5 years or more. The holding period begins January 1 of the year a contribution is made to any Roth IRA.

Traditional IRA

Traditional IRA has some similar features to Roth IRA. The contribution limit is the same as Roth IRA which is $7,000 for under 50 age and $8,000 for age 50 or older for the year 2024. Remember the contribution limit is a combined total for both Traditional and Roth IRA, meaning you can contribute $2,000 to Traditional and $5,000 to Roth for a total of $7,000 or you can contribute the total limit to either a Traditional or Roth IRA. Also, you must have earned income in order to contribute.

The contribution and any gains inside the Traditional IRA are tax-deferred until withdrawn at retirement. The contribution amounts for Traditional IRA are tax deductible in the year of contribution. However, the amount of tax deduction might be limited or reduced if you or your spouse are covered by a retirement plan at work and your Modified AGI is over a certain amount. If neither of you have retirement plans at work, then the contribution is fully deductible if you fall under a certain Modified AGI amount.

Please see the table (2024) below if you are covered by a plan at work.

If you're covered by a retirement plan at work, use this table to determine if your modified AGI affects the amount of your deduction.

If your filing status is...	And your modified AGI is...	Then you can take...
single or head of household	$77,000 or less	a full deduction up to the amount of your contribution limit.
single or head of household	more than $77,000 but less than $87,000	a partial deduction.
single or head of household	$87,000 or more	no deduction.
married filing jointly or qualifying widow(er)	$123,000 or less	a full deduction up to the amount of your contribution limit.
married filing jointly or qualifying widow(er)	more than $123,000 but less than $143,000	a partial deduction.
married filing jointly or qualifying widow(er)	$143,000 or more	no deduction.
married filing separately	less than $10,000	a partial deduction.
married filing separately	$10,000 or more	no deduction.

If you file separately and did not live with your spouse at any time during the year, your IRA deduction is determined under the "single" filing status.

Source: www.irs.gov

Please see this table (2024) below if you are NOT covered by a plan at work.

If you're not covered by a retirement plan at work, use this table to determine if your modified AGI affects the amount of your deduction.

If your filing status is...	And your modified AGI is...	Then you can take...
single, head of household, or qualifying widow(er)	any amount	a full deduction up to the amount of your contribution limit.
married filing jointly or separately with a spouse who is not covered by a plan at work	any amount	a full deduction up to the amount of your contribution limit.
married filing jointly with a spouse who is covered by a plan at work	$230,000 or less	a full deduction up to the amount of your contribution limit.
married filing jointly with a spouse who is covered by a plan at work	more than $230,000 but less than $240,000	a partial deduction.
married filing jointly with a spouse who is covered by a plan at work	$240,000 or more	no deduction.
married filing separately with a spouse who is covered by a plan at work	less than $10,000	a partial deduction.
married filing separately with a spouse who is covered by a plan at work	$10,000 or more	no deduction.

If you file separately and did not live with your spouse at any time during the year, your IRA deduction is determined under the "single" filing status.

Source: www.irs.gov

401(k)

Most of you probably heard about 401(k) at your workplace. 401(k) is a type of retirement plan offered by your employer where the employee contributes a percentage of their salary or wage to the plan. The contribution is a pre-tax amount which means it's excluded in the calculation of how much tax is deducted from your paycheck.

The contribution limit for 2024 is $23,000. If you're 50 or older, you can contribute an additional $7,500. Employers often offer matching contributions as an incentive. Something to remember is that the combined employee and employer contributions cannot be more than $69,000 or $76,500 if you're older than 50 and also cannot be more than the employee's compensation.

Most employers have a vesting period requirement for matching contributions' portion. For example, a company might require you to stay with the company for 3 or 5 years to be fully vested. Your own contribution will always be 100% vested.

The IRS doesn't allow you to keep the retirement fund in your account indefinitely. There is a minimum withdrawal requirement once you reach the age of 73. According to the IRS, "If you don't take any distributions, or if the distributions are not large enough, you may have to pay a 50% excise tax on the amount not distributed as required."

In general, withdrawals or distributions from an IRA or retirement plan before the age of 59 ½ are considered early distributions and are subject to a 10% early withdrawal penalty.

However, there are exceptions to avoid the 10% penalty if you fall under one of the following exceptions according to the IRS. See the table below from the IRS website.

Exceptions to the 10% additional tax

Exception	The distribution will NOT be subject to the 10% additional early distribution tax in the following circumstances:	Qualified plans (401(k), etc.)	IRA, SEP, SIMPLE IRA* and SARSEP plans	Internal Revenue Code section(s)
Age	after participant/IRA owner reaches age 59½	yes	yes	72(t)(2)(A)(i)
Automatic enrollment	permissive withdrawals from a plan with auto enrollment features	yes	yes for SIMPLE IRAs and SARSEPs	414(w)(1)(B)
Birth or adoption	distributions up to $5,000 per child for qualified birth or adoption expenses	yes	yes	72(t)(2)(H)
Corrective distributions	corrective distributions (and associated earnings) of excess contributions and min aggregate cover … and excess deferrals, made timely	yes	n/a	401(k)(8)(D), 401(m)(6)(A), 402(g)(2)(C)
Death	after death of the participant/IRA owner	yes	yes	72(t)(2)(A)(ii)
Disability	total and permanent disability of the participant, IRA owner	yes	yes	72(t)(2)(A)(iii)
Disaster recovery distribution	up to $22,000 to qualified individuals who sustain an economic loss by reason of a federally declared disaster where they live	yes	yes	72(t)(2)(M), 72(t)(11)
Domestic abuse victim distribution	to a victim of domestic abuse by a spouse or domestic partner, up to the lesser of $10,000 or 50% of account, distributions made after 12/31/2023	yes	yes	72(t)(2)(K)
Domestic relations	to an alternate payee under a Qualified Domestic Relations Order	yes	n/a	72(t)(2)(C)
Education	qualified higher education expenses	—	yes	72(t)(2)(E)
Emergency personal expense	one distribution per calendar year for personal or family emergency expenses, up to the lesser of $1,000 or account balance decreased …	yes	yes	72(t)(2)(I)
Emergency savings account	distributions from a pension-linked emergency savings account 12/31/2023 …	yes	—	402A(e)(1)
Equal payments	series of substantially equal payments	yes	yes	72(t)(2)(A)(iv)
ESOP	dividend pass through paid from and ESOP	yes	n/a	72(t)(2)(A)(vi)
Homebuyers	qualified first-time homebuyers, up to $10,000	no	yes	72(t)(2)(F)
Levy	from plan of IRS levy of the plan	yes	yes	72(t)(2)(A)(vii)
Medical	amount of unreimbursed medical expenses (>7.5% AGI)	yes	yes	72(t)(2)(B)
Medical	health insurance premiums paid while unemployed	—	yes	72(t)(2)(D)
Military	certain distributions to reservists while serving …	yes	yes	72(t)(2)(G)
Returned distributions	…	n/a	yes	408(d)(4)
Rollovers	in-plan Roth rollovers or eligible distributions contributed to another retirement plan or IRA within 60 days (also 72(t) features of the 60 day rollover distributions)	yes	yes	402(c), 403(a)(4), 403(b)(8), 408(d)(3), 408A(d)(3), 457(e)(16)
Separation from service	the employee separates from service during or after the year the employee reaches age 55, for public safety employees of a state or political subdivision in a state, or a governmental tax exempt benefit or defined contribution plan	yes	no	72(t)(2)(A)(v), 72(t)(10)
Terminal illness	distributions made to a terminally ill employee, on or after the date the employee has been certified by a physician as having a terminal illness	yes	n/a	72(t)(2)(L)
Unemployed health insurance	distributions equal to the amount paid for health insurance by an individuals as well as unemployed for 12 weeks and received unemployment compensation in the year of the distribution or the subsequent year	n/a	yes	72(t)(2)(D)

Source: www.irs.gov

Rollovers of Retirement Plans and IRA Distributions

People often change jobs for various reasons such as for better salary, work environment, or move to a different state. So, what do you do with the 401(k) or other retirement plans with your former employer?

There are a few options you can take such as a lump-sum distribution or rollover to another IRA. With lump-sum distribution, the amount is taxable and may be subject to withholding and an additional 10% penalty for early distribution. To avoid that, you can do a direct rollover to another retirement or IRA account. You have 60 days to do a rollover. For additional details, please visit the IRS website. www.irs.gov

Backdoor Roth IRA via Conversion

What is a backdoor Roth IRA you might wonder? Since the Roth IRA has an income limitation rule, many high-income earners can't contribute to it. To get around this rule, many people use the strategy of converting a regular IRA or 401(k) to a Roth IRA because there are no income limitations for conversions nor how much you can convert. You can convert all or part of your traditional IRA or 401(k) to a Roth IRA. It is all totally legal. However, the conversion has to be completed within the 60-day period.

For example, you changed jobs, and you wanted to rollover your 401(k) from your former employer to another IRA. Instead of rolling it over to another regular IRA, you can choose to roll it over to a Roth IRA instead. **However, one important thing to remember is that you have to pay taxes on the amount you rolled over.** It could create a huge tax liability, so careful consideration is needed before considering the conversion.

Why do people choose to do that and what are the benefits you might ask? Simple. **The money that grows inside the Roth IRA is tax-free no matter the size when you withdraw after reaching age 59 ½, and you held the account for 5 years or more.** Think about the story I mentioned earlier regarding how Peter Thiel grew his Roth IRA account to $5 billion dollars. If he decides to withdraw all the money after reaching the age of 59 1/2, all of it will be tax-free. You can do the same with your Roth IRA, maybe not $5 billion but certainly can grow your account substantially over time.

Another benefit is Roth IRAs are exempt from required minimum distribution (RMD), which means you can leave the funds in the account for as long as you live. You can also leave your Roth IRA with your heirs when you name them as beneficiaries. However, the heirs must withdraw all of the money within 10 years from date when inherited. To qualify for tax-free withdrawal, the Roth IRA account must have existed for at least five years prior to the account owner's death.

So, **why don't more people do it?** The answer might be **because of the upfront tax liability it creates.** When you convert any amount from a regular IRA or 401(k) to a Roth IRA, you have to pay taxes on it now. The conversion could create a huge tax liability. This strategy might not be suitable or beneficial to some people. Also, the conversion is not reversible. Please talk to your financial advisor to see if this strategy is right for you before making any conversion decisions.

As a reminder, all the information mentioned here can be found on the IRS website. I encourage you to check out their website at www.irs.gov to get more detailed and in-depth information on the topics mentioned here.

It's always a good idea to talk to your financial advisors regarding your financial decisions. What I presented here is for educational purposes only and not financial advice.

Chapter 12

Stock Investing 101 and Tax Strategies

Stock Investing

When it comes to stock investing, one name comes to mind, and that is Warren Buffet, the legendary investor, businessman, and philanthropist. What makes him such a successful investor? What is his secret sauce? What can we learn from him?

Here is some background information I read and gathered from Investopedia about him. According to Investopedia, Warren Buffet started investing at a very early age. He bought his first stock at the age of 11, and his first real estate investment at the age of 14. While pursuing a business degree at Columbia University, he studied under the guide of legendary value investor Benjamin Graham (Dolan, 2024).

He is known as the "Oracle of Omaha" for his investment prowess. He and his best friend, Charlie Munger teamed up to buy the ailing Berkshire

Hathaway textile company which later to be used as a vehicle to acquire other businesses and make investments. Warren Buffet has a keen sense of finding and buying underpriced but solid companies and holding them for the long-term. His current fortune is estimated to be over $140 billion dollars according to *Forbes*.

Some of Warren Buffet's famous quotes are: "Don't invest in something you don't understand", "Invest in companies you believe in", "Be fearful when others are greedy and to be greedy only when others are fearful", "Rule number 1: Never lose money. Rule number 2: Never forget rule number 1", and many other famous quotes by him (Investing Answers, 2021).

What I gather from reading about him and his investment wisdom is that self-education is key. He has said that he reads a lot. He studies many companies' financials to find companies that are solid, have growth potential, and which he believes is currently underpriced to invest in.

In the age of technology, information is readily available on the internet and in many forms of media. Educating yourself in all aspects of investing is the best investment you can make for yourself. The stock market has created many successful multi-millionaires. You too can create and build wealth through stock investment, thus providing a better future for yourself and your family.

However, something important to keep in mind is that stock investing involves risk. The risk is that you could potentially lose your investments. So, know your risk tolerance and only invest the amount that you can afford to lose. Meaning don't use your rent money to invest, because the risk of losing it all is a real possibility.

On the other side of the coin, investing can be rewarding and can build wealth, if you pick solid and reputable companies to invest in which are considered more stable and less risky. The stock market historically has shown on average about a 10% return.

What are some important things you should learn and know before making any investments? Let's go over some things about the stock market.

The stock market is where public companies' stocks are traded. When you purchase a share of stock of a company, it represents a share of ownership. For example, if you buy 100 shares of Apple then you own a fraction of the percentage of the company out of the millions of shares available.

The two major stock exchanges in the United States are the New York Stock Exchange (NYSE) and National Association of Securities Dealers (NASDAQ). There are other exchanges, but I will only focus on these two major ones where the majority of the stocks are traded and listed.

The highest chance of success is picking solid and reputable companies. Don't pick companies based on their stock price or invest in penny stocks. When I first started my stock investing journey, I made those same mistakes such as buying penny stock companies thinking because they are cheap, well these companies' stocks are cheap for a reason. The chance of these penny stock companies going bankrupt is high. So, don't pick stocks solely on the price. Learn to analyze a company's financial statements to get a better picture of the financial health of a company.

Also, we can't always time the market to our favor, using dollar-cost-averaging (DCA) is a good strategy to employ, meaning invest at regular intervals regardless of price. In the long run, it will average out the stock's cost basis per share.

Factors Affecting the Financial Market

There are many factors that could have a potential effect on the market and stock price movements at any given time. For example, beware of potential news that's coming out that might impact the market such as when the U.S. Federal Reserve has scheduled meetings coming up, release of Consumer Price Index (CPI) Report, Producer Price Index (PPI), Unemployment data and Job Reports, Inflation Rate, current and future Interest rates, housing market, consumer spendings habits, domestic and foreign policies, etc.

Factors that have an impact on a particular stock are earning release dates and any positive or negative news regarding the company such as mergers or acquisitions, etc. Also, the market and industry trend of the stock segment could have an impact on the stock price movement as well. To make better decisions as an informed investor, you need to pay attention to all these factors.

So, how do you start your investing journey if you haven't already done so? First by opening a brokerage account with any of the brokerages available such as Charles Schwab, Fidelity, Interactive Brokers, E*Trade, or Robinhood. You can open an account with as little as $100, some even have no minimum requirements. If you're brand new to investing, I found Robinhood's platform or app is more beginner friendly than the others.

As mentioned before, when it comes to deciding what stocks to invest in, picking solid and reputable company stock is a safer bet and reduces your risk of losing a huge chunk of your investment. These stocks might have slower growth but still offer a good return on your investment. Know your risk tolerance.

Of course, if you have a high-risk tolerance, you can invest in something riskier but offer higher rewards. It all depends on your risk tolerance.

Type of Companies and Market Capitalization

The stock market is made up of many types of companies from different industries and has different market capitalization. Industries such as technology, services, retail, construction, healthcare, energy, etc.

It is also further categorized according to their size of market capitalization such as small-cap, mid-cap, and large-cap. The term "cap" stands for "market capitalization". Market capitalization is computed by multiplying the share price by the number of a company's outstanding shares (Rosenberg, 2023).

Small-caps are companies with a market capitalization of less than $2 Billion.

Mid-caps are companies with a market capitalization between $2 Billion and $10 Billion.

Large-caps are companies with a market capitalization of $10 Billion or more.

Why does the market capitalization of a company matter? It matters because there's a certain risk level associated with the company's size of market capitalization. Small-cap stocks or companies tend to be more volatile and riskier (Rosenberg, 2023).

On the other hand, large-cap stocks or companies tend to be more stable and usually have been around for a longer period and have name and brand recognition such as Apple, Google, Amazon, etc.

Stocks with Dividends

When it comes to stock investing, some people specifically look for stocks that offer cash dividends. A cash dividend is a distribution of funds or money from a company's current earnings or accumulated profits, and it is paid to stockholders based on the number of shares they own at a certain date. Most brokers offer a choice to re-invest that money or just keep it as cash.

Some important things to keep in mind regarding dividends are the dates. There are four important dates regarding dividends. They are the **declared date, ex-date, record date**, and **payment date**.

The declared date is the date when the dividend is declared and the dividend amount, record date, ex-date, and payment date are set.

The ex-date is the date before which an investor must own the stock to receive the dividend. The record date is the date used to determine which shareholder is entitled to the dividend, which is usually recorded two days after the ex-date.

The payment date is the date payment is issued to stockholders who are entitled to the dividend based on the ex-date and it's usually about one month after the record date.

It's very important to understand the ex-date. In order to get the dividend, you must own the stock before the ex-date. For example, if the ex-date is June 15, you must still own this particular stock as of June 14.

Picking stocks that offer dividends is a great strategy to grow your investment account. Take Warren Buffet for example, his favorite stock is The Coca-Cola Company (KO). It currently pays a quarterly dividend of $0.485 per share per the data on its company website as of November 2024. Warren Buffet's company, Berkshire Hathaway, Inc. owns about 400 million shares (Mancini, 2024). Imagine getting $194 million each quarter times 4 equals $776 million for the year from just the dividends plus any increase in value of the stock. That's a staggering amount! As you can see, the power of investing and picking the right stocks. It's life changing wealth.

Well, you might say that you don't have that kind of money to invest. Of course, most of us don't have Warren Buffet kind of money to buy 400 million shares. But we can start small by buying 10 or 100 shares and slowly building up your portfolio over time. Save and set aside money to invest on a regular basis. Make your money work for you.

Tax Treatment of Dividend Income

When you receive a dividend payment, it is either going to be treated as ordinary income or qualified income depending on the length of time you held the underlying security or stock. Qualified dividend is treated at a more favorable rate. To qualify as "qualified dividend", you must own and hold the stock for 60 of the 121 days before the ex-dividend date.

On the 1099-Div form that your financial institutions send to you at the end of the tax year, it will list the amount of dividends in box 1a and 1b. Box 1a is the total dividend you received. Box 1b is the portion out of box 1a that is qualified to be treated as "qualified dividend".

For example, Box 1a, you have $1,500 and Box 1b, you have $800. That means $700 will be taxed as ordinary income while $800 is taxed at a long-term capital gain rate at your income level. See the table below.

2024 Long-Term Capital Gain Tax Rates and Income level

Tax Rate	Single	Married Filing Jointly	Married Filing Separately	Head of Household
0%	$0 - $47,025	$0 - $94,050	$0 - $47,025	$0 - $63,000
15%	$47,026 -$518,900	$94,051 - $583,750	$47,026 - $291,850	$63,001 - $551,350
20%	$518,901 +	$583,751 +	$291,851 +	$551,351 +

Common Pitfalls of Investors

As an investor, we often fall into some common pitfalls due to inexperience or just human nature. I, myself, have made many of these mistakes.

Pitfalls such as not taking profits more often, buying cheap value stocks or penny stocks (solely based on price), fail to limit losses by not placing stop losses, holding on to a certain stock for too long instead of cutting losses, too emotionally attached to a certain stock, not diversifying your portfolio enough or invest heavily into one stock, FOMO (fear of missing out) or chasing risky stocks. Be aware of these pitfalls and take steps to correct or limit them to help you become a better investor.

Tax Strategies for Reducing Capital Gain Taxes

Capital gains are gains from sales of investment assets such as stocks, bonds, real estate, etc. When you sell an asset such as stock for the price less than what you paid for, then you have a gain. For example, you purchased Apple stock (AAPL) for $150 and sold it a year later for $225, then you have a long-term gain of $75. All your gains and losses are netted together to come up with a net total gain or loss. If you have a total net loss, you can deduct up to $3,000 of loss to offset ordinary income each year and the remaining losses are carried over to next year.

For example, you have short-term loss of $2,000 and long-term loss of $8,000, so your total loss is $10,000. You can deduct $3,000 against ordinary income and carry a long-term loss of $7,000 to next year.

There are different tax rates for short-term and long-term gains and how they are treated for tax purposes. Short-term is defined as investment assets held for less than 1 year and is taxed as ordinary income at an individual's regular income tax rate. Long-term is defined as investment assets held for more than a year.

The tax rate for long-term is 0%, 15%, or 20% of the capital gain, depending on the tax filer's income and filing status. Holding investment assets for more than a year is preferred because long-term capital gain tax rates are usually less than ordinary income tax rates.

So, what are some strategies one can employ to reduce your tax liability?

The first one is to hold the assets for more than a year whenever possible. Long-term capital gains have a favorable tax rate than short-term. One of the big advantages of long-term capital gain is that it is totally possible to pay 0% tax on your capital gain if your income level is below a certain amount.

For example, if you and your spouse file a married joint return, and your income is below $94,050 for 2024 and you have a long-term capital gain of $90,000. All of the $90,000 gain is taxes at 0%. So, essentially the $90,000 gain is tax free. In your year-end tax planning strategy, if you currently only have 40,000 gains or even losses, you can sell some of your assets that have substantial gains up to income limit of $94,050 to take advantage of the 0% tax rate each year.

Please see the table below for each income level based on your filing status.

2024 Long-Term Capital Gain Tax Rates and Income level

Tax Rate	Single	Married Filing Jointly	Married Filing Separately	Head of Household
0%	$0 - $47,025	$0 - $94,050	$0 - $47,025	$0 - $63,000
15%	$47,026 -$518,900	$94,051 - $583,750	$47,026 - $291,850	$63,001 - $551,350
20%	$518,901 +	$583,751 +	$291,851 +	$551,351 +

Loss Harvesting

Loss harvesting is another strategy to employ to reduce your taxes. Loss harvesting is when you purposely sell some of your losing assets to offset your gains.

For example, you have accumulated a substantial amount of gains during the year. At year-end, you can sell some of the stocks that have lost a large amount of value, and you know that the price will not go back up again anytime soon. You can use these losses to offset the gains you have, thus reducing your capital gain tax.

Wash-Sale Rule

As an investor, you need to be aware of the wash-sale rule. A wash-sale rule is a rule that prevents you from claiming a loss if you repurchase the same or substantially similar one within 30 days before or 30 days after the sale. The wash-sale rule is a 60-day window period. For example, you sold Apple (AAPL) stock for a loss of ($100) on July 15. Later, you decided to purchase Apple stock again on July 30. Then the $100 loss is disallowed.

Even though the loss is disallowed, the loss is not entirely lost. Instead, the $100 loss is added to the basis of the stock you just bought. Thus, increasing the cost basis of the stock which will reduce your gains when you sell in the future.

Stock Trading Terms Made Popular by Retail Investors

As more and more retail investors come into the market, trading has become more common and popular. From this trend, came the trading slang lingos made popular by the retail investors on platforms and social media such as The WallStreetBets on Reddit, X (formerly Twitter),

Facebook, etc. Below are some popular trading terms or jargon you should know as an informed investor.

FOMO - Fear of Missing Out

YOLO - You Only Live Once (going all in)

HODL – Hold On for Dear Life

To The Moon – Investors often say, "To The Moon", when the price of the asset rises significantly and keeps going up and up.

Whales – Refers to large financial institutions or someone with lots of capital and purchase huge sums of stocks, cryptos, or other securities.

Stonks – An intentional misspelling of the word "Stocks".

Fiats Money – Currency issued by the Government.

Diamond Hands – is used to describe someone planning to hold the asset/stocks for a long time and not planning to sell anytime soon even as the price fluctuates or very volatile.

Paper Hands – is used to describe someone who is very risk averse. This person or investor is selling or closing their positions at first sight of trouble or falling prices.

Bagholder - A bagholder is an investor who is holding on to stocks or positions which the price has fallen significantly from the purchase price.

Pump and Dump – A pump and dump is a scenario where people or a group of people send out false or inflated information or recommendations to boost the price of a particular stock or asset. When the price rises on these assets, the fraudsters then sell off the shares at an inflated price which causes the price to plummet, leaving investors who buy in at a later time with losses or holding the bags.

In summary, stock investment is a great way to build long-term wealth. As with any type of investments, stock investing involves risk, know your risk tolerance, please do your own research and due diligence before investing. All the materials presented here are for educational purposes only and do not constitute financial advice.

Chapter 13

Harness the Power of Option Trading

How does option trading work? Options are financial contracts that give the holder the right to buy or sell a financial instrument such as stocks, funds, commodities, and indexes at a specific price for a certain period of time.

In this chapter, I will specifically focus on the basic form of stock option contracts only. An option is a contract giving the buyer or seller the right, but not the obligation, to buy or sell the underlying asset at a specific price on or before a certain date.

There are three key features of an option contract. They are **strike price, expiration date**, and **option premium.** The strike price is the price at which an option can be exercised. The expiration date is the date at which an option expires and becomes worthless. The option premium is the price you paid to buy the specific option contract. One option contract is equal to 100 shares of the underlying stock or security.

The option's price is simply the premium you paid or get when you buy or sell an option contract. The option's premium is based on many factors, such as strike price, expiration date, volatility of the security and the option Greeks, which I will discuss later.

There are some option terms which describe whether an option is profitable or unprofitable.

At-the-Money (ATM)

When an option is at-the-money, it means that the option's strike price and the underlying asset's price are equal.

In-the-Money (ITM)

When an option is in-the-money, it means the option's strike price is more favorable than the underlying asset's price which resulted in a profit.

Out-of-The-Money (OTM)

When an option is out-of-the-money, it means there's no profit when comparing the option's strike price to the price of the underlying asset.

Intrinsic Value

There's something called intrinsic value in options. An option's intrinsic value is when there's profit existed comparing the strike price and the price of the underlying asset or stock.

Look at the following table:

	At-the-Money (ATM)	In-the-Money (ITM)	Out-of-the Money (OTM)
Call Option	Current Stock Price = Strike Price	Current Stock Price > Strike Price	Current Stock Price < Strike Price
Put Option	Current Stock Price = Strike Price	Current Stock Price < Strike Price	Current Stock Price > Strike Price

There are two types of options: calls and puts. A "call option" is when you bet on the price of the underlying asset to rise. A "put option" is when you bet on the price of the underlying asset will fall.

Call Options

A "call option" gives the holder the right, but not the obligation, to buy or sell the underlying security at the strike price on or before the expiration date.

For example, you purchase an Apple (AAPL) call option on November 18, 2024, with a Strike Price of $230 with expiration date of November 22, for a premium of $1.40. Remember one contract is equal to

100 shares. So, 100 x premium of $1.40 is $140 for this contract.

You have 3 actions you can take as to what to do with this call option.

1. You can close this option any time before November 22.

For example, on November 20, the price of AAPL increased to $240 and the premium has increased to $2.00. You wanted to lock in the profit from the increase in premium. To close, you just do the opposite, which is to sell the call for the exact date and strike price. On your brokerage account for that option contract, you will see a +1 shown on the expiration date and strike price you have selected when you purchase the option.

2. You can do nothing and let it expire worthless.
3. You can exercise your option by buying the underlying asset at the strike price, which is $230 in this example. Remember 1 contract equals 100 shares, so $230 x100 equals $23,000 to exercise this contract.

Put Options

A "put option" is an option contract that gives the holder the right, but not the obligation, to buy or sell the underlying stock at the strike price on or before the expiration date.

A buyer of "put option" is betting on the price of the underlying asset to fall.

A buyer of a "put option" has the same 3 actions they can take as a "call option".

1. They can close any time before the expiration date.
2. They can exercise the option by selling the underlying assets at the strike price.
3. They can let the option expire worthless

In most cases, the majority of people will close out their option contracts before the expiration day.

There are some specific characteristics related to stock options one needs to pay attention to. One of the **most important features** to remember about stock options is the **"Time Decay"** aspect of option contracts.

Time decay means every day the option contract loses value as it nears expiration. Time decay is the rate of change in value to an option's price based on the "Theta" value. For example, an Apple (APPL) call option for strike price of $230 with expiration date of November 22, has a Theta of -.2669. Meaning, every day the premium price is reduced by this rate. An option contract loses value every day (time decaying).

The time decay increases as it is near the expiration date. For an option to be profitable, the increase in price of the underlying security or stock needs to be more than the daily decay.

Theta is just one of the four major Greeks that affect the option's price. The four Greeks are **Delta, Gamma, Theta,** and **Vega** (Summa, 2024).

Delta measures the impact of a change in an option's price (premium) resulting from a change in the underlying security.

Gamma measures the rate of changes in delta over time.

Theta measures the rate of time decay in the value or premium of an option.

Vega measures the risk of changes in implied volatility of the underlying asset price.

One other lesser-known Greek is **Rho**. Rho measures the impact of changes in interest rates on an option's price.

All the Greek values are measured between 0.00 to 1.00 for call options. Theta is always negative between -1.00 to 0.00 for both calls and puts. Theta is used to measure time decay so it's always negative.

In put options: Delta, Theta, and Rho are negative while Gamma and Vega are positive between values 0.00 to 1.00.

Why Trade Options?

What are the reasons why some people choose to trade stock options? There are many reasons as to why one would trade options instead of simply buying the underlying stock or security itself. Options can be used as a hedging strategy, as speculation, or to use it as leverage (Downey, 2024).

Hedging Strategy

When using options as a hedging strategy, the goal is to offset any potential unfavorable moves in the other investments. For example, the options can be used as a hedge against a declining stock market to limit downside losses. One of the main reasons why options were created is to use them as a hedge or insurance to limit losses.

For short sellers, buying call options is a way to limit losses if the underlying stock or security moves substantially higher against their trade, especially during a short squeeze.

What is a short squeeze? Per definition from Investopedia, "A short squeeze happens in financial markets when the price of an asset rises sharply, causing traders who had sold short to close their positions (Mitchell, 2024)."

What conditions create a short squeeze scenario, you might wonder? This usually happens when a stock or security is heavily shorted. When short sellers make their trades expecting that the price of a stock will fall but instead the stock unexpectedly rises sharply in a short period of time, the short-sellers may have to act fast to limit their losses if they continue to go higher and higher.

How it works is that a short seller usually borrows shares of an asset that they believe will drop in price and buy back later for a cheaper price. If the price falls, they are able to buy back the stock for a cheaper price and return the shares and pocket the difference between the price when they initiated the short and the price when they buy back the shares to close the position.

However, when the opposite happens, meaning instead of falling prices, the price keeps rising, which creates a huge loss for the short-sellers. They need to act fast to limit their losses, meaning in order to close the position, they have to buy the stock at whatever the current price is at. If more people are buying the particular stock, it will send the stock price higher and higher, thus creating a short-squeeze situation.

A perfect example of a short squeeze happened in early 2021 to GameStop (GME) stock. Around that time, the world was still under lockdown due to the Covid-19 pandemic. Due to the pandemic, lots of businesses are closed or mandated to close. Many people lose their jobs or work remotely, and people spend more time at home.

Around this time, the government is looking for ways to help people who lose jobs and to stimulate the economy. The government passed stimulus acts to give people free stimulus money based on their filing income and status.

With all this free money, consumers have more money to spend. People are looking for ways to entertain themselves and find things to do with their stimulus money. Around this time, people developed an interest in stock investing. These people are called **retail investors.**

I, myself, have been pretty active in trading during this time and grew my portfolio substantially between 2019 to 2021. I was fully aware of the GameStop short-squeeze saga. I first became aware of this stock when it was under $10. I didn't believe this company was a good company to invest in, so I didn't buy this stock at first. But I keep hearing people talk about it on platforms such as Reddit's r/WallStreetBets, Facebook, X (formerly Twitter). I started to notice that the price keeps going up almost every day. I say to myself, this company is not doing so well. Why are people buying this stock? Eventually, I did buy a few hundred shares of the stock, but I sold them before the short- squeeze happened.

Here's a background story of the GameStop (GME) short squeeze according to an article by "TheStreet" (Salvucci, 2023).

GameStop (NASDAQ: GME) is a video game retailer that operates stores out of malls and shopping centers. Its main business is the sale of games and consoles. By the mid-2010s, GameStop began to lose market share because more people are opting for online games and purchases and also traffic at shopping malls have decreased due to people shifting to online shopping.

GameStop's business was struggling by the end of the decade and the company's stock price has dropped significantly. Many hedge funds and large institutional companies are betting that GameStop will go under soon thus causing the stock price to drop even further by their short selling.

Around this time, the world experiencing a Covid-19 pandemic which shut down much of the retail economy in early 2020 and it seemed GameStop's fate was sealed. However, an army of retail investors came on the scene armed with pandemic stimulus money, unemployment checks, and plenty of free time due to lockdown.

These retail investors collectively decided to invest in this stock and take on the large institutional and Hedge Fund companies to send a message to them. By late January 2021, GameStop's price had skyrocketed to over $500 a share. The hedge fund companies that short GameStop lose billions of dollars. Companies such as Citadel LLC and Melvin Capital. Eventually, Melvin Capital shuts down its business due to the heavy losses sustained during the GameStop short squeeze.

Below is a timeline of the GameStop short squeeze that inspired the "Dumb Money" per the article in the "TheStreet" (Salvucci, 2023).

"June 1, 2019: GameStop Stock closes at around *$7.47* per share.

Mid-2019: Michael Burry's private investment firm, Scion Asset Management, purchases over 3% of

GameStop's outstanding shares, believing the company to be undervalued by the market.

July 31, 2019: *Bloomberg* reports that GameStop's short interest stands at around 57,226,706 of 90,268,940, meaning that over 63% of the company's outstanding shares are currently sold short.

August 16, 2019: Michael Burry personally addresses GameStop's board of directors in a letter, stating that his firm owns "2,750,000 shares, or about 3.05%, of GameStop." Burry expresses "concerns regarding capital management" and urges the company's leadership to continue to use its cash to complete large stock buybacks in order to increase the company's earnings per share.

August 30, 2019: GameStop stock closes at *$3.97* per share.

September 30, 2019: By the end of 2019's third fiscal quarter, the company had repurchased and retired about 34% of its outstanding shares.

December 31, 2019: GameStop stock closes at *$6.08* per share.

July 2020: Keith Gill (Roaring Kitty) begins releasing YouTube videos explaining that he has held a position in GME since mid-2019 (around the same time Burry bought into the company) and believes the company is undervalued and over-shorted. Gill makes the same case on Reddit's r/WallStreetBets as u/DeepF**kingValue.

August 31, 2020: GameStop stock closes at *$6.68* per share.

November 2020: By November 2020, Ryan Cohen, an activist investor known best for his former role as CEO of Chewy, an online pet supply retailer, had purchased over 10% of GameStop's outstanding shares.

November 30, 2020: GameStop Stock closes at *$16.56*.

December 8, 2020: GameStop hosts its Q3 earnings call. The company misses Wall Street revenue estimates due in part to pandemic-related store closures and reports an adjusted net loss of $0.53 per share, causing shares to slide sharply downward in after-hours trading.

4th quarter 2020: At some point during Q4 2020, Michael Burry's Scion Asset Management exited its massive position in GameStop, according to regulatory filings.

January 4, 2021: GameStop stock closes the first day of January trading at *$17.25*.

January 11, 2021: Ryan Cohen, the activist investor who owns over 10% of GME stock, joins the company's board of directors along with Alan Attal and Jim Grube, two e-commerce specialists who also used to work for Chewy.

January 13, 2021: GameStop stock jumps to an intraday high of *$38.65* on the news of Cohen & Co's appointments to the company's board.

January 19, 2021: Citron Research, a prominent GME short seller, tweets that GameStop's retail investors are "suckers at this poker game" and that the stock will fall "back to $20 fast."

January 20, 2021: Citron Research cancels a planned report on short interest in GameStop amid supposed harassment from GME bulls.

January 22, 2021: GME's short interest stands at around 140%, meaning 40% more shares had been sold short than actually existed on the open market. This occurred because shorted shares were re-lent and shorted again. Shares go up by over 50% to close at *$65.01*.

January 25, 2021: Citadel invests $2.75 billion in hedge fund Melvin Capital, which is heavily short on GameStop. More than 175 million GME shares are traded, and the stock closes at *$76.79*.

January 26, 2021: Elon Musk, CEO of Tesla and SpaceX, tweets "Gamestonk!!" and shares a link to r/WallStreetBets, the Reddit message board on which bullish retail investors discuss and promote GME. The stock surges, closing at *$147.98*.

January 27, 2021: Equity and options trading volume in the U.S. reaches its highest-ever single-day level (24.5 billion shares and 57.1 million contracts traded, respectively. GME sees its highest close of the squeeze at *$347.51* after reaching an intraday high of around *$380*.

Melvin Capital and Citron cover most of their short positions at staggering losses.

January 28, 2021: GME reaches a pre-market high of over *$500*. Robinhood, a fee-free trading app popular among GME's army of retail investors (along with several other popular brokerages) halts buying of GameStop stock but continues to allow sell orders), angering investors and prompting suspicions of market manipulation.

GME closes at around *$193.60*. The U.S. Financial Services and Senate Banking Committees plan a hearing for February 18 to discuss the GME phenomenon.

February 2, 2021: Janet Yellen, U.S. Treasury Secretary, requests a meeting of regulators to discuss the volatility created by the recent wave of retail trading. GME closes at *$90*.

February 4, 2021: Robinhood lifts remaining trading restrictions on GME and related stocks. GME closes at *$53.50*.

February 18, 2021: A hearing titled "Game Stopped? Who Wins and Loses When Short Sellers, Social Media, and Retail Investors Collide" is held by the U.S. House.

Robinhood CEO Vlad Tenev speaks, assuring the panel that Robinhood does not have inappropriate relationships with hedge funds, claiming "We don't answer to hedge funds ... we serve millions of small investors who use our platform every day to invest." Tenev claims that trading was halted because the clearinghouses that conduct the actual trades made on the company's app raised their prices.

Keith Gill (AKA Roaring Kitty and u/DeepFuckingValue) speaks, exclaiming, "A few things I am not: I am not a cat. I am not an institutional investor, nor am I a hedge fund." GME closes at *$50.31*.

February 19, 2021: GME falls to its post-squeeze low, closing at *$40.59*.

March 12, 2021: GME reaches a post-squeeze high, closing at *$264.52*.

After March of 2021, GameStop's stock continued to see fairly drastic ups and downs, but none were as stark as January's short squeeze. Overall, the trend was down between early 2021 and late 2023.

The stock remained popular, however, among both retail and institutional investors and among both bulls and bears, seeing higher volume and volatility than it had in the years leading up to 2020.

Whether the company's director shakeup and strategic shift toward digital sales will spell long-term success for the video game retailer remains to be seen (Salvucci, 2023)."

Leverage

Another reason for trading options is leverage. For example, if you want to buy 100 shares of Apple which are currently trading at around $228 dollars. You will need $22,800 dollars. However, you can buy that 100 shares with 1 option contract and pay a premium of $3.55, which comes out to be $3.55 x100 =$355. Remember one option contract equals 100 shares. You can own the same number of shares for $355 compared to $22,800. That's the power of leverage with options.

Manage Your Risk with Option Size Allocation

When investors use options as a leverage tool, sometimes they take on too large of a position on a particular option trade.

For example, some investors are risking 50% or more of their total portfolio on one trade and cross their fingers hoping it will work out in their favor. YOLO as they call it. Unfortunately, if their trade goes against them, they will lose 50% of their portfolio.

Managing option size is the key to long-term investing. You don't want to blow your portfolio in one or two trades and can't come back from it. You should only allocate 10% or 20%, at the most, of your portfolio money to option trading and limit your size on each trade. Know how much you are willing to lose before you make the trade.

Other More Complex Option Strategies

There are many types of option trading strategies besides the simple buy of calls and puts. Depending on your financial goals and risk tolerance and what you're trying to accomplish.

For advanced traders, they can employ many different types of option strategies which require more experience and knowledge, below are some of the strategies one can employ for the experienced traders.

They are:

- Covered Call
- Naked Call
- Married Put
- Bull Call Spread
- Bear Put Spread
- Butterfly Spread
- Straddle (Long)
- Strangle (Long)
- Iron Condor
- Iron Butterfly

If you would like to learn more about these strategies, I encourage you to do your own research and find other resources to learn more about them in greater detail.

The information presented here is for educational purposes only and does not constitute financial advice. Please do your own research and due diligence before making any financial decisions.

Chapter 14

The High Risk and High Reward of Crypto Investing

History of Bitcoin

By now, the majority of you most likely have heard of Cryptocurrency or have some idea of what cryptocurrency is. Cryptocurrency is a form of digital currency. The most widely known cryptocurrency is Bitcoin, and it is the first digital currency that was created and adopted worldwide.

Based on many sources on the internet, Bitcoin was started by someone with the pseudonym of "Satoshi Nakamoto". No one really can confirm who the real person is behind the name Satoshi Nakamoto, to this date it is still unknown.

In August of 2008, he introduced the blockchain system with the release of the Bitcoin whitepaper, titled "Bitcoin: A Peer-to-Peer Electronic Cash System" and was posted to a cryptography mailing list.

According to an article in U.S News, titled "The History of Bitcoin" (Pinkerton, 2024), how Bitcoin started was, "In a 2008 white paper, Bitcoin's enigmatic creator introduced the blockchain system, the backbone of the cryptocurrency market. A blockchain is a digital ledger of transactions replicated and distributed across a network of computer systems, securing the information. It allows any person with internet access to make financial transactions independent of banks, financial firms and the government (Pinkerton, 2024)."

The following are some core concepts regarding Bitcoin and cryptocurrency in general, per the same article in U.S. News, titled "The History of Bitcoin" (Pinkerton, 2024).

"Bitcoin units. Each Bitcoin is divisible to eight decimal places. A millibitcoin (mBTC) is 1/1,000th of a Bitcoin. The smallest unit is a satoshi (sat), which is 1/100,000,000th of a Bitcoin.

Transaction. A computer directive styled as "payer X sends Y Bitcoin to receiver Z."

Block. A block is a group of Bitcoin transactions over a certain period. Transactions are verified by Bitcoin "miners."

Mining. A process where individuals or groups ("miners") solve complex calculations to validate transactions and create new blocks. Miners are financially rewarded for their work with newly minted BTC.

Block hash. Mining activities include a record-keeping service ensuring the blockchain remains consistent, complete and unalterable. The hashes validate available Bitcoin and provide a uniform mining reward.

Blockchain. A continuous, transparent ledger where each block transaction is seamlessly linked to the previous one. This public chain enables both Bitcoin's existence and usability.

Blockchain address. A sequence of 25 to 34 alphanumeric characters used to receive Bitcoin while concealing personally identifiable information. While cryptocurrency exchanges may be required to collect personal data, each transaction can use a different Bitcoin address to enhance privacy.

Keys. Credentials, similar to a safe-deposit box, that allow access to Bitcoin assets. If a party loses their key, the Bitcoin becomes inaccessible and effectively worthless. According to Chainalysis, a blockchain analytics firm, roughly 20% of Bitcoins have been lost due to misplaced private keys.

Public keys. This is the technology used to encrypt and decrypt transactions. It is "one way," allowing transactions to be unlocked but not reversed. This key enables the blockchain to be uninterrupted.

Private keys. A unique passcode used by transacting parties to initiate a Bitcoin transaction. To spend Bitcoin, one must know their own private key and digitally sign the transaction. The party's signature is verified by the public key without revealing the private key. Private keys are invaluable and must be protected. If a party loses their key, the Bitcoin becomes inaccessible and effectively worthless. A 2023 Finbold study showed that 39.7% of individuals had forgotten their passwords (Pinkerton, 2024)."

How is Cryptocurrency Traded ?

Cryptocurrencies can be traded on many crypto exchange platforms such as Coinbase, Binance, Crypto.com, Kraken, etc. These are just some of the major crypto exchanges, there are many others available on the market. Beside Bitcoin, there are many other coins or cryptos available to trade, those are called Altcoins.

Examples of altcoins are Ethereum, Solana, XRP, Dogecoin, Shiba Inu, Pepe, etc. Basically, anything other than Bitcoin is considered altcoins.

The Wild Rides of Meme Coins

Dogecoin, Shiba Inu, and Pepe are considered meme coins. **What is a meme coin?** You might wonder. According to Investopedia, "A meme coin is a cryptocurrency named after characters, individuals, animals, artwork, or anything else in an attempt to be humorous, light-hearted, and attract a user base by promising a fun community (Rosenberg, 2024)."

Most of the meme coins are traded at less than a penny when they are first listed and many still never pass more than a dollar. Meme coins at first seem like such a bad investment. However, meme coins can have the potential of making many people millionaires and it did.

The Rise of DogeCoin

Dogecoin is one of the biggest and oldest meme coins around. Dogecoin was initially started as a joke by software engineers Billy Markus and Jackson Palmer (Wikipedia, 2024).

Many of you might or might not know of the rise of the Dogecoin saga. I myself was very much part of this event as I owned a substantial amount of Dogecoins at the time. The price of Dogecoin started to rise after it was listed on Robinhood, a popular app used by many new retail investors.

At the time, I believe it was trading less than $0.003 or something like that in 2019. If you have invested $10,000 at $0.003 and sold at its peak price of $0.7316 on May 8, 2021. You would have made over $2.4 million dollars.

The rise of Dogecoin's price is mainly due to many new retail investors coming into the market. Dogecoin's popularity was also fueled by Elon Musk, when he mentioned Dogecoin as his favorite meme coin. Many people did become Dogecoin millionaires or made a substantial amount of money overnight during its peak.

However, the price did drop drastically a month after the all-time high and was on a continued decline afterwards. As of November 2024, Dogecoin's price started to move again. Currently, it trades at around half of what the all-time high price was. With the renewed interest in crypto and many positive developments, we can expect to see positive things for the crypto industry in 2025 and beyond.

Cryptocurrency is highly volatile and risky, and the price can fluctuate widely from one moment to the next. Cryptocurrency goes in cycles, there's bull cycle and crypto winter cycle. A winter cycle is when the market is in a long stagnation or price decline. Know your risk tolerance and do your research before investing in any cryptos as it is highly volatile.

Types of Wallets

What is a crypto wallet? According to Blockchain Council (Smith, 2024), "A crypto wallet is used to interact with a Blockchain network. The three major types of crypto wallets are hardware, software, and paper wallets. Based on their work, they can be further classified as cold or hot wallets. Software-based wallets are more accessible and more convenient, whereas hardware ones are the most secure. Paper wallets are printed out on paper and are now unreliable and obsolete. In reality, crypto wallets don't store the currency but act as a tool of interaction with Blockchain, i.e., generating the necessary information to receive and send money via Blockchain transactions.

The information comprises pairs of private and public keys. Based on these keys, an alphanumeric identifier called address is generated. In essence, this address specifies the location to which coins can be sent to the Blockchain. The address can be shared to receive funds, but private keys are to be never disclosed. The private key can be used on any wallet for accessing the cryptocurrency. As long as the private key is known, funds are accessible on any device. Also, coins are just transferred from one address to another, never leaving the Blockchain (Smith, 2024)."

There are two types of wallets. They are either hot wallets or cold wallets. A hot wallet is connected to the internet and is less secure but more user-friendly to use. A cold wallet, on the other hand, is usually a hardware, and is stored offline and doesn't require internet connectivity and is considered more secure. Examples of cold wallets are hardware such as Ledger Nano or Trezor. Examples of hot wallets are desktop wallets, mobile wallets, and web wallets.

Wallets can be further divided into two categories. They are Custodial Wallets and Non-Custodial Wallets. Custodial wallets are wallets that are controlled by a third-party, usually vulnerable to hacks, but more user-friendly.

Examples of custodial wallets are wallets you have with crypto exchanges such as Coinbase, Binance, Kraken, etc. On the other hand, holders of non-custodial wallets have full control of the wallet. It is usually considered more secure and less vulnerable to hacks but usually requires someone to be more tech savvy. Examples of non-custodial wallets are Ledger Nano, Trust Wallet, etc.

Safeguard Your Wallet from Hackers

When you purchase cryptos, you can store them and leave them with the crypto exchanges that you purchase them from, or you can store them in a cold wallet.

However, many crypto investors prefer to self-custody their cryptos with cold storage wallets because it is considered more secure as mentioned in the previous section to prevent their wallets being hacked. Take precautions to protect your wallets. Don't give out your private information, don't click on links asking for your information, don't fall for scams or fall for someone claiming to be from legitimate sources.

Learn and beware of the common scams tactics and methods so you can recognize red flags. Hacking is a real issue in the crypto world. Occasionally, you will hear about someone's account being hacked.

One of the biggest hacking scandals in the crypto world is the story of "Mt. Gox Hack".

Mt. Gox is a bitcoin exchange based in Japan and was one of the largest bitcoin exchanges in the world at the time. Below is the story of how the Mt. Gox Hack unfolded according to an article from "CoinDesk's Consensus Magazine (Wilser, 2023)".

The Mt. Gox exchange first came into the scene in 2010. It was originally created by Jeb McCaleb. The name Mt. Gox came from the fantasy card game "Magic: The Gathering". McCaleb wanted to have a place to buy and sell cards, so he launched Mt. Gox, short for "Magic: The Gathering Online Exchange" (Wilser, 2023).

On the first day of Mt. Gox operations, 20 bitcoins were traded and each cost 5 cents. Back then, there weren't many places for people to trade bitcoins. When Mt. Gox came along, it made trading bitcoin an easier process for many. So, the Mt. Gox exchange grew rapidly in popularity among early bitcoin adopters. Mt. Gox grew so big that it accounts for 70% of all the bitcoin transactions.

In 2011, McCaleb felt frustrated and burdened by running the site, so he sold Mt. Gox to a French coder named Mark Karpeles.

In January 2014, one of the Mt. Gox customers named Burges was traveling with his girlfriend in Paris for his 40th birthday. He tried to cash out and withdraw some of his bitcoins, but it didn't go through. Soon, many other customers encountered the same issue that they were unable to withdraw their bitcoins.

Burges had 250 bitcoins with Mt. Gox and at the time it was worth about a quarter of a million dollars. He was frustrated and wanted to get his bitcoins back. He was determined to get his bitcoins back, so he booked a flight from London to Tokyo. He went to Karpeles' office and staged a protest in front of his office with a big sign that said, "MT. GOX WHERE IS OUR MONEY?" Burges soon caught the attention of a reporter from The Wall Street Journal and a reporter from a new website that covers the crypto space, CoinDesk (Wilser, 2023).

Despite it being a cold and snowy day, Burges waited patiently for Karpeles to show up for work.

When he finally did show up, Burges confronted Karpeles and asked, "Do you still have everyone's bitcoins?"

Karpeles had no adequate answer for Burges. Eventually, the truth came out that Mt. Gox had been hacked. The bitcoins were gone.

In February 2014, during the Tokyo press conference, Karpeles said " We had weakness in our system, and our bitcoins vanished.". He announced that Mt. Gox is ceasing operations and declaring bankruptcy.

It was believed that around 750,000 bitcoins were stolen, that's roughly around 7% of all bitcoins existed at the time. However, later it was able to recover 200,000 bitcoins in one of the old wallets, but the rest still never recovered.

In 2017, a Russian national named Alexander Vinnik was arrested and charged with playing a role in the laundering of the bitcoins stolen from Mt. Gox.

Some positive things did come out of this Mt. Gox hack such as exchanges are now incorporate better security measures such as two-factor authentication,

KYC mandates, and reserve requirements of exchanges.

There is also good news for Mt. Gox customers. In 2019, a rehabilitation program was established to repay the creditors. Given the rise of Bitcoin prices, they are currently much higher than it was in 2014, so it was not all lost for the Mt Gox bitcoin holders, some might be even glad that they were essentially forced to hold the bitcoins until now.

The distribution was originally scheduled to be completed by October 31, 2023, but was extended to October 31, 2024 (Norry, 2023). They have the option of getting the repayment in the form of fiat currency or bitcoin. With the expected continued rise of the price of bitcoin, I suspect many will opt for bitcoin.

The Pros and Cons of Self-Custody Wallets

When it comes to crypto investing, we have to take into consideration such as what platform we use, how do we store our crypto currencies, self-custody or third-party custody, etc.

Given the many stories of crypto wallets being hacked. Many people opt for self-custody with hardware wallets also known as cold wallets. The Pros of self-custody wallets are that you have full control of your wallet and your cryptos. It's considered more secure, less prone to hacks, and also protects your privacy.

However, there are also a few important Cons with self-custody wallets. The number one Con is, you have to safeguard and remember your private key. If you ever lost or don't remember your private key or your seed phrase. You can't access your wallet and those cryptos are forever lost.

A private key is a randomly generated alphanumeric code number. A seed phrase, which is a set of randomly generated words used to create the private key and acts as a backup for enabling wallet restoration and fund access if the original wallet is lost or damaged.

Another con of self-custody is safeguarding your physical hardware wallet. If you lost your hardware that holds your wallet, then it's gone forever.

An example of such a heart-breaking story is the story of a British man named James Howells.

According to an article by CoinDesk (Crawley, 2024), in 2013, James Howell accidentally threw out a hard drive containing 8,000 Bitcoin (BTC). Over the last decade, Howells has made numerous requests to Newport Council, who are the proprietors of the landfill where the hard drive is believed to end up in an attempt to find and retrieve the hard drive but has been unsuccessful in gaining access.

He is now currently suing the council for damages of 495 million pounds ($646 million) according to the article. The case is due to be heard in December of 2024 but "Howells said that his aim is to "leverage" the council into agreeing to the excavation of the site in order to avoid a legal battle (Crawley, 2024)."

Unfortunately, there are countless sad stories such as this one, where the person either forgot their private keys, passwords, or lost the hardware drive all together. That's why self-custody comes with a lot of responsibilities and safeguards you need to take. Self-custody might not be the best option for everyone.

As you can see, in the world of crypto, things are not perfect. Besides safeguarding your crypto wallet, the crypto market is very volatile and can be a risky investment. There are some bad actors in the crypto space where they will rug-pull their investors and run away with your money. On the other hand, crypto investing can be highly rewarding. There are many good cryptos such Bitcoin, Ethereum and many others out there that have the potential to make you a millionaire. Many people did and have become crypto millionaires, especially those early Bitcoin adopters.

Regarding early adopters, I had a chance to be one of those early Bitcoin adopters. Here's my personal story. Back in 2013 is when I first heard about Bitcoin. I attended a Bitcoin conference which I believe was held at McCormick Place in Chicago in 2013.

At the conference, there were many booths from companies that sell mining machines or even some crypto platforms or exchanges were also there.   I don't quite remember all the details. What I did remember was a company offering free $25 worth of bitcoin to sign up with them. I did sign up but for some reason I didn't receive any bitcoin as promised.

At the time, I didn't really understand what Bitcoin really is, nor believe in its potential. Therefore, I just let it go and didn't really think too much about it. It was not until the Robinhood app came along and crypto started to gain traction and more people started to invest in cryptos, that's when I started to pay attention to crypto again.

Currently, I do have a small portfolio invested in cryptos but wish I had invested early on when I first heard about it. Imagine investing $1,000 in Bitcoin back in 2013 and holding up until now November 22, 2024 at this writing, it's trading close to $100,00 per Bitcoin. **Update:** Bitcoin has surpassed $100,000 in December 2024.

But then again, I don't think I or any of the early adopters would have held the Bitcoins all the way until now. I am sure if I had invested early, I would have sold along the way as the price rises and I am sure others would have sold too. Oh well, as the saying goes, hindsight is 20/20. With the current excitement and momentum and wide adoption, I believe there is still a lot of room for growth for Bitcoin as well as all the altcoins and the crypto industry in general.

Like any investments, it involves risk, and cryptocurrency is especially risky and volatile. Before investing in any cryptocurrencies, know your risk tolerance and do your own research. Educate yourself before investing in anything.

Chapter 15

Stable Investments for the Risk Averse

When it comes to investing, not everyone has the same risk tolerance. Depending on your investment goals. Some people are looking for a higher reward thus they're willing to take on more risks. On the other hand, there are people who have a low risk tolerance and are happy to invest in stable investments that offer some returns but not a whole lot of risk.

The following types of investments are considered less risky and offer a more stable income than the typical stock investments.

Bonds

According to Investopedia, " a bond is a fixed-income instrument and investment product where individuals lend money to a government or company at a certain interest rate for an amount of time. The entity repays individuals with interest in addition to the original face value of the bond (Fernando, 2024)."

The terms of a bond usually include the amount, interest payment to bond holder, and maturity date. The maturity date is the date in which the bond principal must be repaid. The interest payment is determined by the coupon rate. The coupon rate is a predetermined interest rate.

Types of Bonds

There are four primary categories of bonds available in the market. They are Corporate Bonds, Municipal Bonds, Government Bonds, and Agency Bonds (Fernando, 2024).

Corporate Bonds are bonds issued by corporations or companies.

Municipal Bonds are bonds issued by states and municipalities. An advantage of municipal bonds is that they are usually tax-free to the investor.

Government Bonds are bonds issued by the U.S. Treasury. If it is a year or less to maturity, they are called "Bills". If the bond is 1 to 10 years to maturity, they are called "Notes". If the government bonds issued with a more than 10 years to maturity, they are called "Bonds".

Agency Bonds are bonds issued by government-affiliated organizations such as Fannie Mae or Freddie Mac.

There are many variations of bonds such as Zero-Coupon Bonds (Z-bonds), Convertible Bonds, Callable Bonds, and Puttable Bonds. I encourage you to learn more about them on your own if you're interested in getting a better understanding of them.

Although bonds are generally considered less risky, they are not without risk, depending on the credit rating of the bonds. Bonds have credit ratings to determine the level of risk. Credit ratings of a bond are determined by credit rating agencies such as Moody's, Standard and Poor's, Fitch Ratings, etc. A credit rating of "AAA" or "AA" are considered high quality bonds. A credit rating of "BB or CCC", etc. are considered low credit quality and commonly referred to as "junk bonds". Junk bonds are considered to have a higher risk of default. Therefore, careful consideration should be given when picking bonds.

Why do corporations or governments issue bonds? Issuing and selling bonds is a way to raise capital to fund business expansions projects, buy equipment, fund school projects, or build roads, etc. In general, the main reason is that it usually has more favorable terms than borrowing from banks.

Bond prices inversely correlated with interest rates. For example, when the interest rate rises, the bond price falls, and vice-versa. Why? Because if the interest rate rises, that means the money in the bank also gets more interest income compared to buying the bond. You can hold the bond to maturity date or can sell and trade in the open market any time up until maturity.

Mutual Funds

A mutual fund is a fund that consists of a pool of different stocks, bonds, or other securities (Hayes, 2024).

Instead of buying a single stock, like Apple. You can buy a mutual fund that contains a mix of tech stocks, such as Apple, Microsoft and stocks from different industries. Investing in mutual funds is a way of diversifying your investment portfolio.

Mutual funds are managed by professional mutual fund managers of a mutual fund company or investment brokerage. A mutual fund manager usually decides what stocks, sectors, or industries to include in the fund's portfolio. Most of the mutual funds are also index funds that mirror the S&P 500 or the Dow Jones Industrial Average (DJIA). They generally have limited risk. It's the main reason why some investors choose mutual funds over other investments.

Mutual funds are also popular with retirement accounts such as employer 401(k)s, IRAs, and investors who are risk averse.

Types of Mutual Funds

Stock Funds

Stock funds are funds that primarily invest in equity or stocks. The funds' name derives from the size of the companies they invest in such as small, mid, or large capitalization. Another way to name the fund is based on an investment approach such as aggressive growth, income-oriented, and value (Hayes, 2024).

Bond Funds

Bond funds are funds that invest in government bonds, corporate bonds, and other debt instruments with the goal of paying a set of rates of return to the shareholders/investors.

Balanced Funds

Balanced funds as the name implies seek to diversify the investment risk by investing across different securities such as stocks, bonds, money market, or other alternative investments.

Index Mutual Funds

Index mutual funds are funds that mirror the performance of a specific index, such as the S&P 500 or the Dow Jones Industrial Average (DJIA).

Income Funds

Income funds are funds that seek to provide a steady income. They primarily invest in government and high-quality corporate debt and usually held to maturity to provide interest income streams.

Money Market Mutual Funds

Money market mutual funds are safe and risk-risk free types of funds that are mostly invested in government Treasury bills or short-term debt instruments.

International Mutual Funds

An international mutual fund or foreign fund is a fund that only invests in assets that are outside an investor's home country. It's considered more volatile depending on the geographical location of the countries.

Regional Mutual Funds

Regional Mutual Funds focus investments on a specific geographic region, such as a country, a continent, or a group of countries. For example, Latin America, or Europe.

Sector and Theme Mutual Funds

Sector mutual funds are funds that invest in a specific sector such as technology, healthcare, retail, etc.

Socially Responsible Mutual Funds

These funds are usually invested in companies that are socially responsible such as green technology, solar power, wind power, renewable energy, recycling, etc.

Mutual Funds vs ETFs

Mutual Funds and ETFs are investment funds that pool together various investment types. However, there are some differences between the two. Mutual funds can only be traded once a day after the market closes (Hayes, 2024).

On the other hand, ETFs are like stocks and can be traded any time during market hours. ETFs offer more flexibility, and real-time pricing. Another difference is the price of ETFs fluctuates throughout the day during market hours. Whereas mutual funds are priced at the end of trading day.

Mutual Fund Fees

The downside of mutual funds is that there are fees charged for managing the mutual fund. There is an annual fee that is charged to cover the fund's operating expenses such as management fees, administrative costs, and marketing expenses. These expenses are expressed as a percentage of the fund's average net assets called expense ratio.

Another fee is the sales charge or loads when you buy or sell shares. Front-end loads are fees for when you buy shares and back-end loads are fees when you sell your shares before a certain date.

Some mutual funds also have redemption fees such as when you sell your shares within a short period, usually 30 to 180 days. However, this fee is limited to 2 % by the U.S. Securities and Exchange Commission (SEC).

Some firms might charge a fee if you fall below a certain minimum account balance or transactions.

Even with all these fees, mutual funds are a great way to have a diversified portfolio and grow your income over time. They are usually relatively safe investment vehicles with steady returns. You can shop around with different mutual fund firms or brokerages and compare fees and quality of funds available.

Saving Accounts

Certificates of Deposit (CDs)

CDs are saving accounts that you usually open with a bank. CDs tend to offer higher interest rates compared to regular savings accounts. If you have a certain amount of money which you know won't need to be withdrawn within the next 3 months or 6 months or a year. CDs are a great way to earn a higher income instead of leaving them in a regular savings account.

However, one important thing to remember about CDs is that the money is locked up according to the CD term period you agree to. For example, a 3-month or 6-month CD. If you withdraw before the locked-up period, there usually is a penalty for withdrawal. CDs interest rates are fixed for the period of the CD. CDs are also federally insured by the FDIC.

Money Market & High-Yield Savings Account

Both the money market and high-yield savings accounts are very similar in that they both offer variable interest rates. Some money markets have features similar to checking accounts such as debit card access. While high-yield savings accounts usually have a withdrawal or transfer limit per month. They are also federally insured by the FDIC.

If you are looking for stable income with not much risk involved, the above-mentioned investment vehicles are great options to consider.

Chapter 16

Money Saving Hacks

We all love to save money or make our dollars go further. When I talk about money saving hacks, I am not talking about not buying coffee at Starbucks or not going out to eat, although these can help.

Credit Cards

The first money saving hack I recommend is paying off your credit card balance each month if you can afford to. Most of the credit cards charge anywhere from 20% to a high of 35%. Your money in the bank pays less than 1% for checking and less than 5% for saving. Even if you can't pay off the entire balance, you can still pay a little extra than the required minimum payment, this will help you pay off the balance faster thus saving you interest charge in the long run.

Mortgage Payments

Same concept as the credit card payment mentioned above. Say you have a 30-year fixed-term mortgage of $400,000 with an interest rate of 8% and monthly payment of $2,935.

Instead of just paying $2,935, you can make an extra $500 or $1,000 payment. The extra payment will apply directly to the principal, thus reducing the principal balance faster, whereas the $2,935 mostly goes towards the interest payment.

If you consistently make extra payments each month to reduce the principal balance, you could potentially pay off your loan in 20 years instead of 30 years depending on how much extra principal payments you made. Using this method, you will save a lot in interest payment over the life-time of the loan.

Get a Lower Interest Rate

This applies to both credit cards and mortgages. For credit cards, if you have been making payments consistently and on time. You can try calling your credit card company and ask for a lower rate than what you are getting now. Most credit card companies will try to offer you a lower rate to keep you if you have been a loyal customer and a history of making payments on time.

As for mortgage, the current interest rates can fluctuate depending on market conditions. If the interest rate happens to go down enough to justify refinancing your mortgage, then shop around to see which bank or company offers the best refinancing terms to refinance your mortgage. Refinancing your mortgage can save you a substantial amount of money in the long run. Make sure to pay attention to the expenses associated with refinancing to see if it makes sense for your situation.

Set-Up Auto Payments

Technology can make our life easier and save us time and money. One such technological innovation is the auto-payment feature. Gone are the days where we had to write checks and go mail them in the post office. Nowadays, you can set-up auto payment for all your bills and expenses such as utility bills, car payments, mortgages payments, your phone bills, basically anything.

Just set them up once and you are good to go. Setting up auto-payment will save you time by not having to do it manually each time. Also, save gas money to the post office and stamps if you mail checks. It also frees up brain power because you don't have to constantly remind yourself to make payments plus you avoid late fees if you tend to be forgetful.

I personally like the auto-payment feature a lot. One thing I do recommend is to check your bank statement regularly to make sure the charges are correct.

Cut Down on Impulse Buying

How often do you buy something and later have buyer's remorse, or does it turn out you don't really like it that much?

Impulse buying is an urge to buy something at the very moment without much thought or planning that goes into it.

For example, you went to a department store with the intention of looking for some luggage for your upcoming trip. While waiting in line to pay for the luggage you saw on the check-out aisle some nice-looking Stanley Tumblers, these tumblers are all the rage on Tik Tok videos, and you decided to get one even though you already have Tumblers at home but a different brand. That's an impulse buy because you have not planned on it.

As a woman, I am guilty of impulse buying when it comes to clothes. I have so many dresses in my closet with   tags still on it. Oftentimes, when we like something or see something we want, the impulse to buy gives us pleasure or a feeling of satisfaction in that moment. However, afterwards, we might have a buyer's remorse and realize that we don't really like it that much or have a need for it.

To cut down on impulse buying tendency, pause and think about it before you buy especially big-ticket items. Ask yourself these questions. Why do I want it? Do I really need it? Is it worth the money? Will it add value to my life? Do I already own something similar?

Taking time to think or pause before buying gives you clarity to see if you really need it or just something nice to have that can be put off for later or not to buy at all. This is not to deny yourself things but rather to use your money wisely and make better financial decisions and keep more of your money for better use.

NOTE FROM THE AUTHOR

Hello, thank you for purchasing and reading my book. I hope you got some valuable information out of it. It's been a very rewarding journey to write this book.

To be honest, in a way, I am writing this book for myself, as well as others who are looking to improve their life. I feel my life is stuck in a state of stagnation and could use some of the strategies, ideas, and advice presented here to give my life a boost.

Things such as taking better care of our health, exercising daily, forming good habits, surrounding ourselves with good and positive people, etc.

Our mind is powerful, taking good care of our mental well-being is very important too.

When we have a healthy dose of self-confidence and self-esteem. We can accomplish and overcome challenges by knowing that we are more than capable of achieving things, which we tend not to give ourselves credit for. Our self-esteem is knowing our self-worth. We are worthy of all the good things such as happiness and success.

Our finances are an important part of our life. Having good financial literacy can help you achieve financial freedom sooner. Start investing as soon as you can but know your risk tolerance.

There are many types of assets or investment vehicles available such as real estate, stocks, bonds, etc. If you have high risk tolerance, you can look into cryptocurrency but know that this type of investment is very risky.

As with any type of investments there's risk involved so make sure you do your own diligence and seek professional advice.

Finally, I wish all my readers good health, peace, and happiness along with achieving financial freedom for you and your family.

P.S. If you find value from this book, **please leave an honest review** on the platform where you purchased it, so more people can benefit from it also. **Thank you in advance.**

ABOUT THE AUTHOR

Cindy L. Lam is a business consultant who also dabbles in stock and cryptocurrency trading. Some of her hobbies include reading, listening to music, dancing, learning new things and exploring new places. She is a firm believer in life-long learning.

Here's a fun fact about the author. She was a former flight attendant based out of LA and NYC for a major U.S. Airline. This was her first job out of college. She did both domestic and international flights. Currently she lives in Chicago, IL.

Contact information:

Email: cindysbookchat@gmail.com

References

Cherry, K. (2023, December 05). *The Brain and Behavior in Psychology*. Retrieved from VeryWellMInd: https://www.verywellmind.com/lesson-three-brain-and-behavior-2795291

Crawley, J. (2024, October 16). *Man Who Accidentally sent $527M in Bitcoins to Dump Sues Local Council to Retrieve Them: Report*. Retrieved from CoinDesk: https://www.coindesk.com/policy/2024/10/14/man-who-accidentally-sent-527m-in-bitcoins-to-dump-sues-local-council-to-retrieve-them-report

Dolan, B. (2024, October 8). *Who is Warren Buffett? How Did He Make His Fortune?* Retrieved from Investopedia: https://www.investopedia.com/articles/financial-theory/08/buffetts-road-to-riches.asp

Downey, L. (2024, November 15). *What is Options Trading? A Beginner's Overview*. Retrieved from Investopedia: https://www.investopedia.com/options-basics-tutorial-4583012

Explore Psychology. (2024, December 2). *Self-Esteem vs. Self-Confidence: Key Differences and Why Both Matter*. Retrieved from Explore Psychology: https://www.explorepsychology.com/self-esteem-vs-self-confidence/

Farivar, C. (2021, June 24). *Billionaire investor Peter Thiel has $5B in his tax-free retirement account, report finds*. Retrieved from NBC News: https://www.nbcnews.com/tech/tech-news/billionaire-investor-peter-thiel-has-5b-his-tax-free-retirement-n1272317

Fernando, J. (2024, May 3). *Bonds: How They Work and How To Invest*. Retrieved from Investopedia: https://www.investopedia.com/terms/b/bond.asp

Hayes, A. (2024, August 28). *What are Mutual Funds and How to Invest in Them?* Retrieved from Investopedia: https://www.investopedia.com/terms/m/mutualfund.asp

Ibe, O. (2023, March 15). *How to Recognize the Signs and Types of Manipulative Behavior*. Retrieved from VeryWellMind: https://www.verywellmind.com/what-is-manipulative-behavior-5220502

Investing Answers. (2021, March 16). *50 Warren Buffett Quotes to Inspire Your Investing*. Retrieved from Investing Answers: https://investinganswers.com/articles/50-warren-buffett-quotes-inspire-your-investing

Jeffrey, S. (2025, January 8). *The Ultimate List of Habits*. Retrieved from CEOsage: https://scottjeffrey.com/list-of-habits/

Kurt, D. (2024, September 9). *Who Created the Roth IRA?* Retrieved from Investopedia: https://www.investopedia.com/who-created-roth-ira-5219885

Mancini, J. (2024, November 21). *Warren Buffett is Set to Collect $776 Million in Coca-Cola Dividends*. Retrieved from Yahoo Finance: https://finance.yahoo.com/news/warren-buffett-set-collect-776-151517549.html

Mitchell, C. (2024, June 22). *Short Squeeze: Definition, Causes, and Examples*. Retrieved from Investopedia: https://www.investopedia.com/terms/s/shortsqueeze.asp

Murphy, T. F. (2024, March 27). *Self-Discipline*. Retrieved from Psychology Fanatic: https://psychologyfanatic.com/self-discipline/

Norry, A. (2023, November 9). *The History of the Mt Gox Hack: Bitcoin's Biggest Heist*. Retrieved from Blockonomi: https://blockonomi.com/mt-gox-hack/

Pinkerton, J. (2024, October 23). *The History of Bitcoin*. Retrieved from U.S. News: https://money.usnews.com/investing/articles/the-history-of-bitcoin

Rosenberg, E. (2023, June 12). *Large cap vs. Mid Cap vs. Small cap stocks - balance your portfolio for the long run*. Retrieved from Money Wise: https://moneywise.com/investing/stocks/small-vs-mid-vs-large-cap-stocks

Rosenberg, E. (2024, September 1). *Meme Coins: What They Are, Examples, Pros and Cons*. Retrieved from Investopedia: https://www.investopedia.com/meme-coin-6750312

Rosenberg, E. (2024, September 1). *Meme Coins: What They Are, Examples, Pros and Cons*. Retrieved from Investopedia: https://www.investopedia.com/meme-coin-6750312

Sabater, V. (2023, October 26). *How Does the Human MInd Work?* Retrieved from Exploring Your MInd: https://exploringyourmind.com/how-does-the-human-mind-work/

Salvucci, J. (2023, September 15). *An in-depth timeline of the GamsStop short squeeze saga*. Retrieved from TheStreet: https://www.thestreet.com/investing/stocks/a-timeline-of-the-gamestop-short-squeeze

Smith, A. (2024, September 19). *Types of Crypto Wallets| Bitcoin Wallets*. Retrieved from Blockchain Council: https://www.blockchain-council.org/blockchain/types-of-crypto-wallets-explained/

Summa, J. (2024, April 16). *Option Greeks: The 4 Factors to Measure Risk*. Retrieved from Investopedia: https://www.investopedia.com/trading/getting-to-know-the-greeks/

WebMD Editorial. (2023, March 30). *Narcissism: Symptoms and Signs*. Retrieved from WebMD: https://www.webmd.com/mental-health/narcissism-symptoms-signs

Wikipedia. (2024, December 1). *Dogecoin*. Retrieved from Wikipedia: https://en.wikipedia.org/wiki/Dogecoin

Wikipedia. (2024, December 1). *Rockefeller Family*. Retrieved from Wikipedia: https://en.wikipedia.org/wiki/Rockefeller_family

Wilser, J. (2023, May 8). *CoinDesk Turns 10: The Legacy of Mt. Gox - Why Bitcoin's Greatest Hack Still Matters*. Retrieved from CoinDesk - Consensus Magazine: https://www.coindesk.com/consensus-magazine/2023/05/04/the-legacy-of-mt-gox-why-bitcoins-greatest-hack-still-matters